Cybersecurity Leadership
Powering the Modern Organization

MANSUR HASIB, D.Sc., CISSP, PMP, CPHIMS

About the Cover

This is the Crested Giant Saguaro at the Desert Botanical Garden, Phoenix, Arizona, USA as she stood on December 9, 2012 when I first came upon her. She is not an ordinary cactus tree but a giant saguaro – a very special breed of giant cacti found only in the southwestern part of the USA and parts of Mexico. The Saguaro National Forest near Tucson, Arizona is full of these amazing giants. These cacti have some amazing characteristics. They live several hundred years. They mature slowly and deliberately. Their first arms appear in about 50 to 60 years. People have personified and revered them for thousands of years. There are many legends and stories about them.

Though each saguaro is unique, this one is even more special. Only one in about 200,000 saguaros develop a crested arm. Though many theories abound, no one knows why this happens. This is the only giant crested saguaro in this garden. When I came upon this graceful giant, I was awe struck. I spent a long time contemplating her sturdy beauty and grace. I felt that this giant crested saguaro represents to me what leadership is all about. Although this cactus lives in a forest with other distinguished giants – where every saguaro is unique and distinct in their own way – this particular one has found a way to learn something and to do something which distinguishes her even further. She has developed a crest that no one else in that garden has!

She is subtle about it. She blends in among the hundreds of other giant saguaros. Many people will pass by and never see her unique qualities. She gives shelter to woodpeckers and other little birds just like everyone else. She silently endures the harsh dry desert conditions just like everyone around her. She does not complain about her problems. Instead she solves them. She stores water in her giant body. She protects herself from deer and other animals with her sharp pointed thorns – just like everyone else.

She has spread her shallow roots far and wide to quickly capture the little moisture that the sparse rainfalls bring each year. Her roots intertwine with the roots of all the other cacti around her. Together they provide each other the stability and strength they all need to support their tall stature.

She flowers gracefully and bears fruit just like a dutiful member of her flock. Yet, she is an inspiration for all other giant saguaros around her. She is a lucky find for the people who are careful to observe. She reaches for the sky tall and proud – and her elegant beauty is difficult to capture in a single photo frame. She motivates others to be even better than they think they are capable of. She encourages us all to develop a crest for ourselves and to do something more meaningful with our lives. What an awesome example of leadership! And that is why she is the only one special enough to be on the cover of my book on leadership!

Third Edition, September 2015

Published in the United States of America by Tomorrow's Strategy Today, LLC

ISBN: 1502312115
ISBN-13: 978-1502312112

DEDICATION

This book is dedicated to all my friends and co-workers. All of you taught me something about leadership. I am thankful for the bond and memories we share.

I specially treasure the amazing number of people with high integrity, ethics, and leadership qualities who worked on my teams. It was my pleasure and privilege to work with you. You taught me what true leadership and teamwork is all about. You were leaders when you needed to be and followers when you needed to be. You solved problems and issues without ever being asked. Your focus was on the solution rather than the assignment of blame. You utilized the talents of other team members to improve the quality of your projects. You learned from and supported your team members and provided constructive feedback and mentorship. Your main focus was the success of the organization – and you never worried about who got credit. You took ownership of issues, made decisions, planned how to recover from errors, pointed out problems and solutions, took pride in the quality of your work, innovated at every opportunity and ensured the satisfaction of our clients.

You made work and life fun for me. Each of you have perennially occupied a special place in my heart. You have validated my belief that everyone can be a leader.

ACKNOWLEDGEMENTS

Special thanks to my dear friend for over forty years, Shah M. Hasan, Provost at Virginia International University, Ohio for sparking my passion in the art of leadership during our early teens. Our experiments running the school newspaper Chit Chat at Notre Dame College and the youth organization Centurions International as businesses, and all our deep conversations over the years were instrumental in shaping my inclusive leadership style. Since the days of walking over to the USIS library till today, thanks for pointing out all the leadership books I should read.

Thanks to my friend Kevin Zachery for analyzing my team and leadership styles. Your deep insight and advice has been amazing for us. Your book *The Leadership Catalyst*, finally gave me the term to describe exactly what I have always believed a leader to be – someone who inspires and supports everyone to perform at their highest capability possible – while allowing everyone to form bonds, have fun, and enjoy the experience.

Special thanks to some very special people who actively supported my efforts throughout my professional career in information technology leadership: Dean Duncan, Bob Brookshire, Valerie Nash, Hortensia Avina, Patrick South, Mark Kestler, Bill Tsai, Jim Redmond, Matt Henson, Chris Mann, Tom Hogevoll, Barbara Lawson, Jerry King, Celeste Revander-Brown, Toby Ford, Cindy Billovits, Kate Van Name, Rick Langdon, Collin Smith, Sam Sibanda, Regina Denton-Clowser, Joy Horton, Judith Mutinda, Lea Tunajek, Michal Tunajek, Phil Larson, Liz Linton, Regina Gachuhi, Steve Litzenberger, Wynona China, Asiya Cleaveland, Wayne Johnson, Robert Johnson, Shirley Brooks, Catherine Nganga and Wakili Olayiwola.

TABLE OF CONTENTS

About The Book

Based on the constructive feedback of esteemed reviewers who reviewed the first edition a thoroughly revised 2nd edition was published in late 2014. Chapters were added, consolidated, removed and reorganized. This edition provides an index. This book provides a business level understanding of cybersecurity and explains how to lead cybersecurity in any organization. The book also provides a broad understanding of health information technology and cybersecurity in healthcare. It is a valuable resource for executives, students, or anyone interested in gaining an understanding of the field. The book does not require any prior technical or cybersecurity knowledge.

Technology drives the mission of modern organizations today. Cybersecurity strategy has become synonymous with enterprise technology strategy just as technology strategy has become synonymous with organizational strategy. A cohesive implementation of cybersecurity is critical for organizations; it can mean the difference between staying in business and thriving or becoming extinct and irrelevant. Such a strategy can be a hallmark of distinction and a powerful driver of productivity and innovation in an organization.

This book is as much a book on leadership of people in general as it is about cybersecurity leadership. The leadership principles are applicable in any organization. The interconnected articles provide progressive elaboration on the themes of leadership, ethical leadership, and the human governance aspects of leading cybersecurity. These are practical insights from my experience, observations, and research in technology and cybersecurity powered organizational transformations in a wide range of industries such as energy, education, biotechnology, and healthcare.

Most cybersecurity books are written at a very technical level and targeted towards cybersecurity professionals. This book is not technical at all. Articles are short and easy to read. Organizational executives should be able to use the book as a handy checklist to help them lead cybersecurity in their organizations. All students whether high school, undergraduate, or graduate, will find the concepts in this book easy to understand and useful. It will also help anyone explore the inter-disciplinary nature of cybersecurity and figure out if this is a field they wish to get into.

Cybersecurity

Technology drives the mission of the modern organization. Technology which was initially used in accounting, finance, human resources and payroll is so pervasive in every organization today that it has become core to the business. Technology is transforming almost every business sector. Forward thinking organizations and leaders are using technology and cybersecurity to distinguish their organizations and propel their businesses to unimaginable new heights. Technology is reducing healthcare costs, increasing access, increasing transparency, and improving quality at a dramatic pace.

Technology is also pervasive in our personal lives. Technology which was expensive and inaccessible to the masses has become inexpensive, powerful, and consumerized. The usual barriers of access and cost for both hardware and software have vanished. High quality technology is available at low or no cost. Technology is even redefining the human social experience. Countless people forge global bonds, maintain far flung relationships, and communicate, engage, and influence millions of others instantly through technology. Life without technology is unimaginable.

The Cybersecurity Model

In such an environment, confidentiality, integrity, and availability of technology, and information systems have become crucial to our work and personal lives. Maximizing confidentiality, integrity, and availability is the primary goal of cybersecurity.

Confidentiality ensures that people who are supposed to have access to information are the only people who have access to that information. Integrity ensures that information can be trusted – and that no one has manipulated it; information can be traced back to the source, and information can be relied upon to make decisions. Availability ensures that information can be accessed by the people who are supposed to access it, from the locations planned, and for the duration planned.

These goals were first identified in the classic John McCumber (1991) model of information security, which was an important early conceptual model. This model identified three key tools: technology, policy and process, and training and awareness. The model was replaced in 2001 by the

Maconachy, Schou, Ragsdale, and Welch model of information assurance. This model introduced two key points.

First, information security is not a state but a process. In other words, the security posture of any organization must improve perennially over time. Second, training and awareness is not sufficient – people controls (Hasib, 2013) or a systematic management of people for the purposes of information security is required. Subsequent researchers connected such governance and leadership of cybersecurity to the development of a cybersecurity culture (Corriss, 2010; Brady, 2010; Hasib, 2013). These scholars argue that culture governs behavior more than anything else.

The Maconachy et al. (2001) model includes authentication and non-repudiation as two additional goals or characteristics. Authentication is a component of confidentiality which ensures that people who should have access to information and systems have a mechanism to demonstrate they have such authorization. Non-repudiation similarly is a component of integrity which enables information to be attributed to a legitimate source and can therefore be trusted.

Once the Privacy Act of 1974 and the Health Insurance Portability and Accountability Act (HIPAA) of 1996 were introduced, the term privacy as a legal concept was introduced into the cybersecurity vernacular. However, privacy is an aspect of confidentiality. These and other subsequent laws created legislatively protected categories of information and granted privacy rights to members of the public.

However, for the cybersecurity professional, privacy falls in the realm of confidentiality. The key difference is that confidentiality of legally protected information is accompanied by legal compliance requirements, disclosure rules, and timetables in the event of a compromise, and penalties for non-compliance and lack of demonstrable efforts to comply.

As a practitioner, I always focused my technology strategy to the mission of the organization. I used a simple principle: Do nothing to hurt the mission of the organization, and do not block anything which will further the mission of the organization. In addition, due to practical and financial limitations I calculated business risks and prioritized projects and expenses based upon a risk analysis and a strategic vision which spanned several years.

Although the Maconachy et al. (2001) model has been a very helpful teaching model, the model is strengthened once we recognize that mission, risk and governance are essential foundations of the model. During 2014, I made several conference presentations attended by both academic and business professionals and discussed these enhancements with both cybersecurity and non-cybersecurity professionals. Everyone agreed that once these elements are added to the model, we have a holistic cybersecurity model which is easily understood by everyone.

CYBERSECURITY MODEL 2014

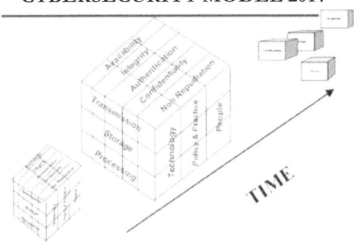

FOUNDATION: MISSION, RISK, and GOVERNANCE

Note. Adapted from "A Model for Information Assurance: An Integrated Approach," by W. V. Maconachy, C. D. Schou, D. Ragsdale, and D. Welch, 2001, June. Paper presented at the 2001 IEEE Workshop on Information Assurance and Security, United States Military Academy, West Point, New York: New York..

We can therefore define cybersecurity in the following manner: Cybersecurity is the mission-focused and risk-optimized governance of information, which maximizes confidentiality, integrity, and availability using a balanced mix of people, policy, and technology, while perennially improving over time.

Cybersecurity and Information Assurance

The term cybersecurity comes from the marketing world. Marketing professionals frequently use buzzwords, such as cybersecurity, advanced persistent threats, data loss prevention, securing big data, securing the cloud, and securing mobile, without ever providing any holistic definition. Sometimes they narrowly define a word to suit whatever technology they are selling – leading business executives to believe that cybersecurity entails pure technology.

Billions of dollars worth of network protection technology have been successfully sold this way. Perhaps this is why the word 'cybersecurity' has been historically associated with technology and the protection of networks. But this is also what has caused serious confusion and the haphazard implementation of cybersecurity in the business environment.

Protection of the network through technology is only one aspect of cybersecurity. What about threats from inside the organization? What about the behavior of people within the organization? What happens when the same people work outside the perimeter of the organization? Is there such a thing called a perimeter anymore?

Let us understand the concept better by applying cybersecurity concepts to the protection of our home. If we focus all our efforts on one main window or door of the house, perhaps on the ground floor, easily accessible to the external miscreant, then our strategy will be highly deficient. Although it may be important to fortify a particular entry point with extraordinary levels of protection, we cannot ignore other aspects of our home.

We cannot ignore the behavior of the people living inside the house or all the people we have provided keys and access codes to our homes. What precautions do these people use with their access? Do they all know how to arm and use the home security, or what to do in the event of any emergency? Have we done drills to ensure everyone will know how to react quickly during a crisis? How will we deal with false alarms? A holistic cybersecurity program protects the whole house; it includes ensuring safe behavior of the people associated with the home.

The meaning of the words cybersecurity and information assurance are coalescing into one comprehensive modern meaning. Due to the universal word recognition and marketing panache, the word cybersecurity has replaced the academic term information assurance. The doctoral program in Information Assurance I completed in 2013 is being renamed to Cybersecurity. Many other schools have already completed this transition. We all need to recognize and embrace this transition.

As we transition, however, we need to ensure that our academic programs in cybersecurity adopt a holistic cybersecurity teaching model. If we lean too heavily on the technical side, or we do not teach all aspects of the modern cybersecurity model to our students and practitioners, our academic program will be deficient.

When organizations implement cybersecurity, they need to base their strategy on a holistic model and a proper definition of cybersecurity as well. Without a proper definition and a holistic model, an organizational cybersecurity strategy will be deficient. We must ensure that our model and definition does not take us back to 1991 and the John McCumber model of information security.

Cybersecurity Leadership is a Business Discipline

Cybersecurity problems are not uni-dimensional; we cannot solve them with one-dimensional approaches. We need a multi-disciplinary, multi-dimensional approach -- and that is what cybersecurity leadership is. The cybersecurity leader must understand the business.

Risk management and strategic prioritization of expenditures are key features permeating such a strategy. Cybersecurity leaders focus on risk opportunities as well as threats. A balanced implementation of cybersecurity increases worker productivity and innovation in an organization. This is because, in order to engage people in a cybersecurity strategy, we need to give them better training on technology they use regularly, and we need to empower them to use that technology more effectively.

Cybersecurity is thus a revenue driver as well as a loss mitigation strategy. Cybersecurity is not a technology discipline; it is a business discipline. All business school programs should include a course in cybersecurity leadership. Historically, some cybersecurity programs focused solely on the technical aspects of cybersecurity. This approach may be okay for training practitioners who wish to focus solely on the technical aspects. However, comprehensive cybersecurity programs should focus holistically on technology, policy, and people. Aspects of business leadership should be included in every cybersecurity training program.

The Role of Senior Executives in Cybersecurity Leadership

Business executives are very familiar with business risk management. Unfortunately by viewing cybersecurity as a technology problem, many senior executives have not embraced their role in the leadership and management of cybersecurity. Chief Executive Officers, C-suite executives, business leaders, corporate boards, and general workers in organizations need to view cybersecurity as their responsibility. Successful cybersecurity leadership starts at the highest executive levels of an organization.

Senior executives also need to view technology as a core component of their business. Information assets are the life blood of most organizations. Technology failures and improper management of risk to technology and systems could drive an organization out of business. Even if something does not cause an outright business failure, prevention is always far less expensive than the actual business and reputation costs of a breach. If cybersecurity can drive an organization out of business, it should be treated as an essential component of the business.

In this new world, organizational leaders also need to recognize that everyone is a technology worker and every company is a technology company. Most business projects today are technology projects. Cybersecurity strategy is usually the business strategy itself. Therefore it is essential for Chief Executive Officers, boards, and other senior business leaders of organizations to understand how to lead cybersecurity. Such an understanding will help them hire the right people and set up the right organizational structure to make their businesses successful.

Budgets

Cybersecurity has to be baked into the entire thinking process of the organization. It needs to be integral to the inception of every information system project. It is difficult to imagine how a separate budget for cybersecurity would work. Such separation would make cybersecurity a separate activity performed by specialists -- after a system is implemented. This practice is very dangerous.

We can have a separate quality control and testing unit or even an auditing unit. But cybersecurity is integral to information technology and its budgeting should never be separated from the information technology budget. Such integration will allow appropriate prioritization of resources and spending according to the strategic initiatives of the organization.

A Human Problem Needs a Human Solution

Organizational leaders also need to remember that despite all the technology, humans are essential to the business. We are all leading humans – and we can never lose sight of that. Cybersecurity is substantially a human issue and much less a technology issue. Human problems need human solutions and a keen understanding of how humans behave. Humans are also the key to innovation and productivity in any organization. Workers of a company are its assets – not expenses. As assets they should be developed, nurtured, trained, and retained because they become more valuable over time. They also need to be utilized effectively.

Many organizations fail to engage everyone in the organization in a virtuous cycle of innovation and improvement, which is essential for cybersecurity. Everyone uses technology and everyone handles data. Some technology departments have viewed governance as a control issue. These departments have focused on controlling everything and restricting users in their use of technology.

Such a control regime has created a trust divide between users and technology managers. It has also restricted the ability of users to use technology effectively – hampering their productivity, and reducing their overall understanding and knowledge of risks associated with the technology and data they handle every day.

Instead of focusing on training users effectively on all the technology and data they use, organizations have spent time and money on cybersecurity awareness programs based on the outdated John McCumber model of 1991. Unfortunately, these programs are still pervasive and pernicious in many corporate environments. Users view them as a necessary evil – but they have no choice in the matter. They waste countless hours, go through lengthy online and in-person training programs, and even suffer through various embarrassing phishing tests -- without any appreciable improvement in their behavior.

The users remain unengaged in the actual improvement of the cybersecurity environment. They do not contribute ideas or point out flaws because they have never been incentivized to do so. However the solution of a human problem has to be a human one. This is why we need leadership – cybersecurity leadership.

Cybersecurity leadership embraces all the people in an organization as the primary key to perpetual excellence in cybersecurity. Such leadership recognizes that innovation is not the sole responsibility of a few anointed people in the organization; innovation is the responsibility of every member of the organization. These leaders provide more technology training – specific to the job requirements of various users – not cybersecurity awareness training. These leaders teach people how to learn on their own. These leaders give people better control over technology and more information about the technology they use.

We need to ensure that people can use technology properly and are trained in advanced self-help techniques because people's work and personal lives have become blurred. Technology has freed up many people from having to go to work because they can work from wherever they are. Global and virtual teams and meetings have become common and pervasive. It has also become highly unwieldy and impractical for people to carry multiple devices – one for work and one for personal use.

Ethical Leadership and Cybersecurity

Declining ethical leadership in an organization is directly related to weak cybersecurity. If the workers of an organization have an antagonistic relationship with the executives and managers of an organization, it will become very difficult to maintain and improve cybersecurity over time. Decline in worker retention and loyalty will lead to intellectual capital loss as well as reduced cybersecurity for the organization. Worker vigilance, innovation, productivity, and loyalty are key factors that guard against insider threats – both accidental and malicious acts.

It is also vital for organizations to maintain their reputations of public trust. When the public entrusts an organization with their personal and confidential information, executives of that organization must embrace the protection of that information as their sacred duty and a moral imperative. Without public trust a company may be able to retain customers when there is no competition; long-term this is a precarious way to conduct business.

Organizations usually exist to provide a public good or a service that consumers want. While profitability is essential for any business, maximizing short-term gains for shareholders, by foregoing appropriate investments or laying off workers annually, should not trump the organization's mission of providing a public good. Although shareholders may gain in the short term, they can get wiped out completely if the business fails. Shareholders and boards should seek ethical executive leaders for long term sustainability and better cybersecurity of organizations.

Organizational Leadership

Many studies of leadership portray leaders as special people, anointed by divinity, in possession of some special power or a collection of traits which cause others to be drawn to them. These views place leaders on lofty social pedestals and suggest that leaders must achieve spectacular and timeless results. Nothing could be further from the truth!

Leadership is the simple act of guiding others towards a purpose. A child guiding her parent to the restroom at her elementary school is performing a leadership act just as chief executives guiding their organizations through turbulent economic conditions. Everyone can use some unique knowledge, ability or skill to guide others. Thus anyone can be a leader.

People are often unaware of their leadership skills and perform below their potential because they are socialized into believing they are followers. They may equate leadership with a position and may wait for cues from this position to perform their duties. Decisions in organizations which adhere to this culture flow up to the anointed leaders. These anointed leaders become single points of failure because they are frequently unqualified to make the right decision.

Value Driven Leadership

Good leaders nurture leadership in others and unleash performance at increasingly higher levels by identifying and focusing on a carefully-chosen set of core values. These values define the actions of leaders as well as their organizations. These organizations benefit from the collective brainpower of all its members instead of the brainpower of a few anointed leaders. My chosen set of leadership values are: integrity, empowerment, teamwork, customer service, continuous learning, and positive reinforcement.

Integrity

Integrity is doing the right thing when no one is looking. Integrity takes a lifetime to achieve but can be lost in a moment. Integrity requires people to always work in the best interests of the organization and the community they serve. People of integrity are committed to their jobs, work with minimal supervision and take pride in what they do.

Empowerment

Empowerment allows key decisions to be made by the person most qualified to make the decision – usually at the lowest possible level of the organization rather than at the highest. Thus decisions are made by people closest to the problem and with the best understanding of the issue. This value unleashes powerful levels of productivity, energy, and innovation within an organization because people feel that they matter. Empowerment fosters self-confidence and the organization solves more problems simultaneously. It reduces more risks in an organization because everyone is engaged in assessing the risk of each action with a questioning attitude. People are not penalized for questioning orders if they believe the orders diminish the safety of the organization.

Teamwork

Teamwork is the magic potion which allows ordinary people to achieve extraordinary results. Good teams have diverse skills and each member is a leader and an expert in something. Members lead in some aspects and follow in other aspects. They know each other's strengths and understand how each role contributes to the success of the organization. Team members hone their leadership skills within the trusted environment of the team. Instead of competing against each other, competition is defined as each member trying to do better each day compared to how they performed in the past. Frank and free discussions and constructive criticism is encouraged and each innovative idea is refined until a team decision with the best mitigation of risk is reached.

Customer Service

Happy customers ensure demand for services, which translates into job security. Customer requirements are understood clearly by asking probing questions. Even if someone asks for a product, we must learn the business purpose to ensure that we meet that purpose. Given limited resources, we must negotiate realistic expectations, including the scope and delivery schedule for the request. We must explain and promptly rectify any unplanned deviations from an agreement.

Continuous Improvement

Quality improvement is automatic when every person in an organization focuses on continuous improvement and demonstrates a willingness to take calculated risks with innovative ideas. A reasonable portion of the organization's resources must be spent on research and innovation. Continuous improvement is another key to job security because it spurs innovation and obviates obsolescence. Within the protected environment of the team, members learn new skills often by partnering with experienced members. They learn with a questioning attitude and a fresh set of eyes, always looking for ways to improve the process.

Positive Reinforcement

Positive reinforcement creates an environment where people enjoy coming to work because they feel their work is valuable. They build symbiotic relationships with others and develop a sense of loyalty to the organization. Having fun at work is important. When people enjoy work, they are more productive. Positive reinforcement is best created with non-monetary rewards. Though we have a limited supply of monetary rewards, we have an unlimited supply of non-monetary rewards. We must celebrate not just successes; we need to celebrate, discuss, and learn from innovative failures. Absence of such a culture will stifle risk taking and innovation.

Final Thoughts

By leading teams using variations of these leadership values in five different organizations over the last thirty years in both public and private sectors, I found everyone has leadership capabilities. Except for a couple of people, whom I had to remove because they lacked integrity and were unwilling to adopt a framework of values, all others on my teams, when provided an environment to innovate, create, grow and make remarkable contributions to the organization, did so with relish and built remarkable careers for themselves. Leadership values served as a powerful framework and created self-propelled leaders out of these people and this made my job easy. The journey has been exceptionally enjoyable for me and all the people I have been fortunate enough to work with.

Connection between Leadership and Ethics

History has provided us with countless examples of leaders. Some like Gandhi and Dr. King achieved immortality and admiration through the greatness of their deeds as they led people towards noble goals. Others like Hitler and Jim Jones (of Guyana) achieved perennial ignominy through the sheer horror of their deeds as they led their followers towards dastardly goals and destruction.

This raises two major questions. 1) Are leaders inherently good or inherently evil? 2) What causes some leaders to be good while others to be evil? We can answer this question by examining the leadership of two leaders: Lt. Colonel Hal Moore from the movie *We Were Soldiers* (Davey, McEveety, & Wallace, 2002) and Willie Stark from the movie *All the King's Men* (Rossen, 1949).

Leadership by itself is neither good nor evil. Leadership is simply the ability to guide others and the act of leading others towards a goal. In practicing leadership, some leaders genuinely have the best interests of others in mind, while others are tangentially interested in the welfare of others while being primarily interested in promoting and preserving themselves at all costs. Some leaders believe in following a righteous path to success while others believe ends justify the means and will stop at nothing, regardless of their legality or morality, to attain their goal. This is why ethics becomes a very important factor among leaders.

A key distinguishing factor good leaders possess is a well developed internal barometer of values and ethics, which guides their leadership style and channels their actions towards doing the right thing at all times. People who do not possess a well developed moral compass, lack this ability to focus on the right things. When these people attain high positions of leadership and power they become highly dangerous to themselves and to others.

The Good Leader: Lt. Colonel Hal Moore

Lt. Colonel Hal Moore (henceforth referred to as Moore) was an ethical leader and his moral compass was clearly evident in his resounding words, "… when we go into battle, I will be the first to set foot on the field and I will be the last to step off and I will leave no one behind ... dead or alive we will all come home together." Chosen to lead a team of ground troops on a helicopter mission into Vietnam, Moore immediately started to recruit good leaders around him and started to train his people for the mission.

He believed in teamwork and wanted his people to train for success. He attempted to make his team stronger by planning for depth and succession. He ordered everyone to learn the job of the person above as well as the person below him. He wanted to lead by example and he wanted others to inspire people into action. He reminded his people that their mutual interdependence was the key to their success.

He shared examples from history such as the story of native American leader Crazy Horse who was suckled by every woman in his tribe in order to reinforce the fact that everyone needed to act as one. He also ensured that his leaders were empowered to lead. He stressed the fact that color, race, religion or other factors were not important. Everyone on his team had to realize that they were on the same team and their survival depended on each other.

Moore knew that he may have been sent on an impossible mission and his troop size was not proportional to the danger and uncertainty they were headed into. However, instead of sulking about things he could not control, he focused on things he could control. That is the mark of a true leader.

He studied the war and the enemy to the extent that he could. He drew from history and his own inner ethical barometer to ensure that he would do everything within his power to preserve the safety of his people and he would not remove himself from the battle scene to save his own life while the lives of his people remained in peril. He made bold promises and kept his word. In praying, he prayed for his people and not for himself.

He was also a loving husband and a devoted parent who cared for his wife and children. He tailored his communications to suit the audience. In speeches to his troops, he spoke of valor, honor and teamwork; yet when he spoke to his children, he explained difficult concepts, such as war, in words they would understand. He was not overly strict in having his children practice every religious ritual perfectly. He comforted his troops as well as his children and allayed their fears. In order to avoid a painful goodbye, he kissed his sleeping wife in the deep of the night and went off to war.

During the war, as morale started to ebb and everyone became concerned about the lack of backup troops, Moore went around complimenting everyone, including his leaders, on the great job they were doing. When US napalm bombs accidentally hit his soldiers on the ground, he knew there could be panic and chaos. Yet, he needed his remaining troops to concentrate on their job at hand.

Thus, he ordered everyone to pick up the wounded to take them to the helicopters. When the helicopters finally came to take them back, he let his men board first. Though he was offered an opportunity to be airlifted out to safety on the first helicopter that arrived in the morning after a devastating firefight, he objected to the order and resolutely stated that he was not going to abandon his people in the middle of a fight.

He was fair and reasonable. He was committed to the well-being of his people. He was honest and clear about the dangers his team was facing. While he was not completely clear on the reasons for going into war, he was able to translate the goals of the mission in a way that his troops could comprehend and accept as a shared goal. His goal was simply to ensure that everyone was brought back home safely – dead or alive. The goal was practical. It established the right tone for the team, and was certainly ethical and honorable. The entire team could benefit from achieving it.

Certainly his team could feel good about it. He and his troops were focused on this goal. He did not abandon his people even though he had the opportunity. He did not expose his people to danger he was unwilling to face himself. His moral conviction on doing the right thing was so strong that he risked his own career and possible retribution for insubordination. He was a good leader and it was his strong ethical barometer that guided him as he performed his duty with a high degree of moral integrity.

He also showed a healthy respect for the dead enemy soldiers. His genuine love for his own men was on poignant display at the end as he reflected on his own survival and lamented that he had survived while his men had died. He tried to soften the pain of war widows by writing to them and by consoling them as he spoke admiringly of the bravery of their loved ones. In summary, Moore was an exemplary ethical leader whose actions would be respected and revered for a long time.

The Evil Leader: Governor Willie Stark

The story of Governor Willie Stark (henceforth referred to as Stark) is a remarkable contrast in leadership. Stark tried to build his reputation as an honest man with courage when he first ran for public office. He campaigned by exposing the corruption and cronyism of the establishment politicians in office. He appeared to have noble goals and displayed some level of empathy for his fellow humans. He even adopted his neighbor's son. However he had a single-minded focus on running and winning.

Even though his professed goal may have been to share the truth with the people, he betrayed his lack of commitment to this goal by half-heartedly agreeing with his wife when she directly asked him if this was his goal. Throughout the entire time, Stark's true goal was self-aggrandizement and he saw himself as a potential Governor and even a President. Because he did not really believe in what he was saying to the people, his passion did not come through in his speeches and he suffered debilitating losses at the elections. His devoted wife helped him to study law and Stark became a successful lawyer by using his aggressive style to convince people that they needed his legal services.

A twist of fate caused several factors to manifest themselves at the same time. First a school building, which was constructed poorly by corrupt politicians and their cronies who were trading favors, collapsed and killed several children. Second, Stark was approached to run for Governor in order to split the rustic vote in favor of another candidate who was unpopular with this segment of the population. Though Stark was unaware of this ulterior motive, he resumed campaigning in earnest.

However he continued to lack passion for the words he was mouthing during his speeches resulting in continued lukewarm support in the early part of his campaign. He had big ideas. But his speeches were prepared and sanitary. Finally in a drunken stupor after the realization that he had been set up to fail, Stark found his passionate voice and started to speak from his heart. This time he sounded as though he truly believed in what he was saying. His speeches finally started to draw people to him.

Though he still lost a close election to a strong establishment candidate, Stark learned from this experience that in addition to a winning message he needed funding and an organization in order to win a state-wide election. In attaining this, Stark resorted to the very corrupt tactics that he had been criticizing -- thus compromising his integrity.

His belief was that he needed to make a pact with the devil in order to carry out his program and win the election. He focused on finding money, buying people and making deals. He believed that the ends justified the means. He professed vociferously that there was evil all around and the only way to achieve something good was to make it out of the bad.

After finally winning the governorship using his new tactics, Stark did provide many beneficial goods and services for the people of his State. However, everything was done to promote his image and immortality. He lacked the humility of a true leader. Stark's rise to power further corrupted him. He even relinquished his fidelity to his wife and succumbed to a series of sexual liaisons – all while making false promises of romance and marriage to young impressionable women.

Everywhere Stark went, he left a trail of evil and corruption. He mistreated the very people around him who had helped him succeed. He tormented and terrorized them by taking advantage of every possible piece of information about them as leverage and by exploiting each weakness they possessed in order to get his way. He did not care about the destruction to their lives as long as it assured his own success and safety. Everyone was disposable and dispensable after they had served his purpose.

When he started to lose people around him, Stark resorted to bribe, extortion, misrepresentation of facts, and even murder in order to protect the professed untainted sanctity of his own reputation. Towards the end when other politicians realized how corrupt Stark had been, Stark found himself entrapped in a web that threatened to bring him down through impeachment.

This is when Stark laid bare his raw cowardice and willingness to sacrifice anyone and to do anything to save himself. He even used his family as a prop for pictures in order to maintain the farce of being a family man to the general public. He conveniently discarded women he was having affairs with as soon as he felt that they were a danger to his public image.

In the end, to people who knew Stark, his reputation changed from being an honest man with courage to someone solely focused on his own needs – someone feeding his own oversized ego and incorrigible insatiable desires. Stark thus became the epitome of a corrupt and evil leader and he started to lose the allegiance of the people around him. Stark's actions showed that he lacked a moral compass. There was no framework of ethics to guide his actions and he lacked integrity.

Final Thoughts

In order to guide decisions, all humans need to have a moral compass so they can weigh each course of action against this moral compass. Such a moral compass will guide leaders to do the right thing when they are faced with a moral dilemma. Moore and Stark were two very different leaders. From analyzing their actions we are able to empirically observe how ethics and integrity can provide a critical internal barometer for guiding our actions and distinguishing between right and wrong. These two examples of leadership help us understand that inherently leadership is neither good nor evil. The possession of a strong moral compass in the form of ethics is the key ingredient which makes some leaders good. The absence of such a moral compass makes other leaders evil.

Profiting through Ethical Leadership

The concepts of ethics and legality can sometimes be confusing. Even though ethics can be a basis for laws, many laws are created with political purposes in mind – to achieve goals that may or may not be ethical. Unfair or unethical laws are often created to justify and to make unethical behavior socially acceptable and legal. For example, slavery was legal in the United States for a long time; women were not allowed to vote.

The law simply states what is lawful and not necessarily what is right. Ethics is an internal barometer which allows us to judge what is right and what is wrong. Though the law may change with time and place, ethics rarely changes. Business organizations want their employees to be ethical and spend resources to reinforce this concept among employees. Organizations also claim to conduct business ethically and purport to treat their customers fairly.

The events of September 11, 2001 presented an unprecedented ethical challenge to the business leaders of the airline industry. From Jim Parker's own lecture (Parker. 2010) and his book *Do the Right Thing* (Parker, 2008) as well as other publicly available material, we can highlight the ethical business decisions of Jim Parker, Chief Executive Officer (CEO) of Southwest Airlines at that time, and the highly positive business impact these decisions had on Southwest Airlines.

Actions of Competing Airline CEOs after 9/11

Immediately following the events of 9/11, all airlines were forced to keep their airplanes grounded. There was panic throughout the United States. Many people cancelled flights and asked for refunds. Most airlines immediately announced plans for eliminating routes and implementing massive layoffs – most with very little compensation or consideration for the employees. Some CEOs made decisions to lay off people simply because others had made the decision to do so and they did not wish to appear foolish to their peers.

Many airlines used little known emergency policies and rules such as *force majeure*, which releases a party from its contractual obligations, to deny laid-off workers severance pay in accordance with their labor union contracts.

In explaining his decisions to lay off 24% of his employees and to invoke the *force majeure* clause, former US Airways President Rakesh Gangwal stated "…the events of September 11th have opened doors for the company that were pretty much closed before (Barakat, 2001)".

Most of these actions were morally wrong and unquestionably unethical and showed little regard for employees or customers and over the course of time, the human and economic consequences of these actions were rather severe for the CEOs themselves as well as for their organizations. The leadership of US Airways was replaced in 2002 and the company suffered massive financial losses in the quarter that immediately followed 9/11 (Barakat, 2001; Gitell, Cameron & Lim, 2005).

Actions of Jim Parker, CEO of Southwest Airlines after 9/11

Southwest Airlines had adopted the ethical practice of *doing the right thing* as a business model from its very inception. The management of the organization had driven this value throughout the organization ensuring that every employee understood it and lived by it. Over the years leading to the crisis of 9/11 Southwest employees had built a remarkable relationship with the customers by practicing this value. Thus, Jim Parker thought through things differently.

He fully expected his customers to cancel flights and ask for refunds. He was well aware that other airline companies were laying off employees in droves, reducing routes and using legal maneuvers to avoid paying severance pay and other benefits to the employees they were laying off. It appeared to him that organizations were taking advantage of the crisis to negate union contracts.

Jim Parker reasoned that in the short term, these decisions were intended to conserve cash. However, in the long-term these decisions were likely to have many unintended consequences and could turn out to be disastrous business decisions. The United States was already experiencing an economic retrenchment following the "dot-com crash".

Letting employees go when they had done nothing to deserve the fate appeared wrong. Letting them go in the face of an economic crisis could not be right for them or for the economy. Denying them severance pay in accordance with their contract was morally wrong. In addition, the message it would send to the employees about their worth to the company could be devastating to the company.

While layoffs may appear to be the short-term panacea for risk management, readily available as a simple management tool, a crisis was precisely the time for leaders to rise to the occasion to make tough decisions that were morally grounded and aimed at the long-term welfare of the organization, its employees and its customers. A crisis was the time when Southwest needed its employees the most. This was precisely when they needed their employees to be highly energized, innovative, and compassionate to customer needs. Jim Parker's ethical barometer told him to do the right thing for his employees.

Jim Parker believed that doing the right thing for his employees and his customers would ultimately be the right thing for his company. He met with the President of Southwest and other leaders and discussed the financial state of the organization and contemplated various risk management options. The team of leaders recognized that if the wave of customer requests for refunds materialized, the company could have difficulty paying employees. They discussed layoffs, grounding planes, cancelling routes and the consequences of these various actions.

However, throughout their entire discussion, the leadership kept focus on one key question: What was the right thing to do? Jim Parker and his leadership team were keenly aware of what the employees meant to the company. They were a vital asset to the organization. They had driven the culture of doing the right thing throughout the organization. It was the culture that defined the entire leadership as well as the employees of Southwest. Employees had built their legendary brand. Employee commitment, engagement and innovation had been the hallmark of the success of the company.

Customer relationships had been built through employees and if anyone could coax Southwest customers into flying again, it would be the employees. Though reducing employees may appear to be a promising option in the short-term, it would destroy allegiance, reduce the productivity of the remaining employees and send the wrong message about the company to both employees and customers. Employees should not be treated as an expense. It could not be logical to callously discard their best assets. A layoff would destroy the long-term prospects for the company.

Thus Jim Parker and his leadership team made a series of tough decisions based on the principle of doing the right thing. As Jim Parker states, "in the absence of any real information, we simply decided to follow our gut and do what we perceived to be the right thing" (Parker, 2008, p. 18). First, they decided not to layoff or furlough any employees. Jim Parker also made the decision to pay employees $179.8 million dollars on the agreed-upon date of September 14, 2001, in accordance with the profit-sharing plan Southwest had implemented in 1973 – the first year that the airline made a profit.

In order to manage cash, pay all the bills on time, and to avoid the possibility that banks would deny him the credit later, Jim Parker drew down on the company's entire $500 million dollar line of credit. He decided not to eliminate routes and did not ground Southwest airplanes. He also decided to unquestionably honor every customer request for a refund. He and his management team went further and promptly announced their decisions and rationale to Southwest employees and customers. They recognized that transparency and honesty about the situation was the best way to engage employees as well as customers into the solution.

In addition they wished to provide clarity during an uncertain period. They wanted to eliminate any lingering layoff fears among the employees so that the employees could fully concentrate on solving the problems at hand. Strategically, Jim Parker also decided to look for opportunities to increase routes and thus create additional short-term and long-term revenue streams for Southwest Airlines while other airlines were giving up on these routes. He felt this was one more right thing for the customer. Flying additional routes would show the customer that Southwest Airlines was ready to serve customer needs at a time when other companies were unwilling or unable to serve them. In order to encourage customers to fly, Jim Parker temporarily reduced the low Southwest fares and made them even more attractive.

Effects of the Decisions

What resulted was remarkable! The wave of customer refund requests never materialized. Certainly there were some who wanted money back. However, most customers who cancelled flights did not want money back. Instead many wrote offering to send money and some actually did. They recounted stories of how Southwest Airlines had touched their lives. The message from the customers was clear. They were going to stand behind the company.

The employees did their share. They innovated and figured out how to solve every problem that came across their way. They reduced operating and maintenance costs dramatically (Brancatelli, 2008). They served customers well beyond the call of duty. One employee drove a customer from Tucson to Phoenix in his personal car to enable the customer to catch a flight. The customer's re-routed flight plan allowed a four hour window; there was no connecting flight from Tucson to Phoenix. However, the drive from Tucson to Phoenix was only two hours.

Lessons Learned

The events of 9/11 had provided Jim Parker and his leadership team at Southwest to test the business profitability of doing the right thing in the face of a remarkable crisis. The results that followed are a testament of the power of this value and how this value can be profitable for a business. As remarkable at it may seem, Southwest Airlines actually made a profit in the quarter following September 11, 2001 and never looked back (Parker, 2008).

Today, almost thirteen years after the tough decisions that Jim Parker and his team made, the results of his long-term wisdom are clearly visible. While almost every carrier in the airline industry has suffered as a result of economic conditions, oil prices and the vagaries of the market, for over thirty years Southwest Airlines has been profitable every quarter of every year (Brancatelli, 2008). Over-reliance on layoffs at other companies have actually precipitated increased financial problems (The Daily Beast, 2010). Some airlines have filed for bankruptcy – American Airlines being the most recent airline to do so.

Yet Southwest has a growth plan of 2 to 3 percent and its market capitalization at \$9.7 billion is higher than the combined \$5.7 billion market cap of its six major competitors (Brancatelli, 2008). Southwest's recent acquisition of AirTran will increase its market share and routes even further (Southwest.com, 2012b). Today, Southwest continues its brand of superior customer service by including check-in baggage fees into the price of their ticket (Southwest.com, 2012a) while most airlines have split up this fee in an effort to generate more revenue at the psychological cost of creating a customer impression that these airlines are more interested in their own revenue and less interested in service to the customer.

The lessons to be learned are valuable. Doing the right thing was highly profitable for Southwest. The company did not exacerbate the national economic problem during the period after 9/11 and has maintained its steady pace during the recent recession. Perhaps as more businesses adopt the practice of doing the right thing, the United States will begin to enjoy a healthier economy with fewer ravaging economic disruptions.

Organizational Values

We can see the power of value driven leadership and ethical leadership. We can see how organizational values define what an organization stands for and how the organization conducts business. Values are the foundation of an organizational culture. Organizational leaders should incorporate the following key values in their organizations to nurture high degrees of productivity and innovation and a strong cybersecurity culture.

- *Integrity and Ethics* – Integrity is doing the right thing when no one is looking. While ethics and integrity can take a lifetime to achieve, they can be lost in a moment. Once lost, they can never be regained.

- *Commitment to the Mission* – Everyone must understand and support the organizational mission. All actions must be in support of the mission and each person needs to understand how their work furthers the mission of the organization.

- *Confidentiality, Integrity, and Availability of Information* – Confidentiality ensures that distribution of information is limited to what is required to provide service. Integrity ensures that the information is trustworthy and free from unauthorized alterations. Availability ensures that the information and systems are accessible to authorized people in the manner planned and during the time periods planned.

- *Transparency* – This value ensures that everyone will be open, honest, and up front in conducting their business.

- *Collaboration* – The organization should believe in the diversity of ideas. The collective brainpower of all people within an organization is stronger that the smartest person in the organization. Thus inclusion of other people and ideas into anyone's projects and engagement in discussions and constructive criticism to refine any idea will ensure that the final product is of a higher quality.

- *Continuous Improvement* – Cybersecurity is not a state – rather it is a continuous process. Therefore, continuous improvement is essential for success. People must educate themselves continuously. They must continuously think of ways to improve the organization, its work processes, and products. They must learn and adopt new technology and engage with their industry peers and other experts by attending and presenting at conferences, by sharing ideas and by learning from others so the organization continues to be among the leaders in its market.

- *Empowerment* – Successful organizations are nimble and make more decisions at any given point in time. Empowerment means that each person will be a leader rather than a follower and take responsibility for actions. People can be leaders in what they do. Leadership does not come from a position. Rather it comes from people becoming aware of the importance of what they do and ensuring that it is done with high quality, pride, and ownership. It also means pointing out deficiencies and the opportunities for improvement. This principle ensures that decisions will be made at the lowest level of the organization possible rather than at the highest level. This will allow more decisions to be made by the organization and result in better quality and more timely service to its clientele.

Convergence and Strategic Leadership Collaboration

Appropriate organizational strategy and cybersecurity leadership requires the highest layers of the executive suite to engage in strategic leadership collaboration. The participation and inclusion of information technology and cybersecurity strategists in these strategic discussions has become vital for organizational success. This is because of the vital role information technology (IT) and cybersecurity plays in the mission of the organization.

In this new world, three areas of an organization which has traditionally been separate have to be merged through strategic collaboration if not through outright departmental merger. These areas are telecommunications, information technology, and facilities or building management systems. The interrelationships, interdependence and cybersecurity implications of these three areas require deep strategic collaboration.

In many organizations telecommunications and IT departments naturally merged as phones became digital and could run on the same physical network infrastructure as the data network. It is rare to see these two departments being run separately today. However the second convergence between facilities, particularly building management systems, and information technology has been going on for a while.

This is because rooms and buildings have become increasingly reliant on technology. Emergence of cybersecurity systems has caused a significant convergence of building security systems, video surveillance, and IT systems. Disaster recovery, business continuity, and incident management must all be planned collaboratively.

Collaboration and communications with workers, business partners, customers, members of the public -- have become extremely important for every organization. Knowledge is growing at an incredible pace. It is impossible to know every aspect of an issue – no matter how smart we are. So, collective wisdom and interdisciplinary solutions have become essential. For almost every problem or issue, there is a need for collaboration and communication. Since global virtual teams have become the norm – when we need an expert in something we can get that expert from anywhere in the world.

This new convergence has impacted the planning of work spaces as well as the technology used in those workspaces. Furniture, lighting, audio, video, comfort systems, safety systems, access control – have become intertwined. Security systems, building access control, ID badges, biometric systems, radiation monitors, body scanners -- all can and are frequently implemented on the same infrastructure and are managed by a unified team. We are also seeing the Internet of Things becoming a reality.

This convergence is accelerated with IT's growing reliance on facilities. Power, furniture – functional and ergonomic, fire suppression, HVAC, monitoring systems, cabling – all require collaborative planning. With limited organizational resources – we cannot afford to waste – and we must do it right the first time. As much as possible, we must plan all possible organizational services on common infrastructure.

Essentially we have an incredibly strong need for three components of an organization to collaborate and plan collectively:

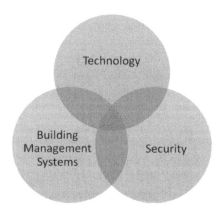

Strategic Collaboration

Although there is a need for collaboration, collaboration is not easy and does not happen automatically. We need to understand how collaboration works and plan for this collaboration. Organizational change can force collaboration – or it can happen organically by people deciding to do the right thing for the organization – through the process of strategic collaboration. This is when organizational leaders from various departments plan the future of the organization together. They develop the best collective solutions for the organization – and not the best solutions for their department or for themselves personally.

Strategic collaboration is not simply a bunch of people working together. These are strategic leaders – very different from each other – who are collectively developing organizational strategy by feeding off of each other. Such collaboration has one key element: Mission of the organization is paramount – everything is planned to ensure that the organizational mission is enhanced.

Spending, changes, vendor selections, transitions, risk management, and many other functions are all planned cooperatively. There is transparent sharing of plans. Since people come from different perspectives, there is a constructive conflict of ideas. These different perspectives are essential. We need people to say that an idea is dumb. There is nothing wrong with having a dumb idea – we all have them – the key is to make sure someone points that out, before we implement the dumb idea. We need to make sure that someone helps us to polish the idea into a brilliant idea. This is what strategic collaboration achieves in an organization.

Expression of dumb ideas should be expected and accepted. Innovative ideas often appear dumb when initially expressed. It becomes harmful only when people have such big egos that they squash constructive criticism and refuse to accept important suggestions, which would transform their dumb ideas into brilliant ones. The final idea should always be a collective idea – one that includes the collective wisdom of all the different perspectives – one that everyone will support. This is strategic collaboration.

We may wonder if the organizational structure is important. Organizational structures can either be a hindrance or a catalyst. However, right leadership and right people are more important than organizational structures. I have experienced strategic collaboration even when facilities, telecommunications and IT were separate departments – simply because we had the right leaders in these organizations. These leaders overcame organizational boundaries for the good of the organization. If we have the wrong people in leadership positions, even a converged organization will not work.

Forced organizational changes with the wrong people in leadership positions can result in several problems: 1) people who would have been successful in separate environments will now be unsuccessful in a converged environment; 2) people may actually start to work against the organizational structure and make it fail; and 3) they may leave.

We must recognize that when we decide to converge organizations and departments, we have to pay attention to the people. People can usually transition – but they may need retraining. They may need leadership coaching and they may need help in learning to operate as a team. They may also need assistants to make up for the skills they do not have.

Paying attention to people is very important in running organizations and planning convergence. We all have feelings, emotions -- normal human qualities and needs. We can put the brightest person in the wrong job and the person will fail. On the other hand, if we put people in positions that are right for them, they will frequently overcome their initial lack of skills – through their sheer passion for the work – which will drive them to learn and excel. The key is to never put people in positions they will not enjoy and do not want to be in. Strategic leadership collaboration at the top executive layers of an organization is vital for success.

Enterprise Cybersecurity Governance

The governance strategy of any organization must focus on the mission. Governance must start at the board, CEO, and at the very highest levels of the organization – not at the lower technical levels. The organization's approach in pursuing the mission must be inclusive and balanced to ensure participation, involvement, and input from all stakeholders. Such inclusion and balance must permeate the organization's governance framework. This framework serves the following purposes:

- Establishes the culture and tone for conduct.
- Specifies the framework for decision making, accountability, and integrity; including roles, responsibilities, and code of conduct.
- Establishes the strategic vision for information technology.
- Encourages and influences everyone to help achieve goals.
- Encourages transparency.
- Aligns risk management with the mission and ensures compliance.
- Ensures due diligence and monitoring of behavior, operations, and managerial practices.
- Ensures effective controls, metrics, and enforcement of policies and decisions.
- Provides clarity and communicates information assurance or cybersecurity policies.
- Makes governance systemic throughout an organization (Westby & Allen, 2007).

We have already stated how cybersecurity or information assurance is the strategic (mission focused) management of information technology and systems which maximizes confidentiality, integrity, and availability of information using a balanced mix of technology, policy, and people while perennially improving over time. Technology and policy are important and required components of cybersecurity. However, a strong focus on people is important (Hasib, 2013) due to the following reasons:

- Research data during the past 5 years show that between 80-90% of security incidents in US healthcare are caused by people inside the organization (Hasib, 2013; HIMSS Analytics, 2008, 2010, 2012; Ponemon Institute, 2009).

- People are the most critical component of a cybersecurity or information assurance program (Maconachy, Schou, Ragsdale, & Welch, 2001).
- People have a behavior choice (Prescott, 2012).
- Technology or policy alone does not govern behavior (White, 2009).
- Culture influences behavior (Corriss, 2010).
- Management engagement at all layers is required for implementing culture (Dutta & McCrohan, 2002; White 2009).
- Support and buy in from people at all layers is required for success (Brown, 2005).

Focus on people has high returns on investment for the following reasons:

- Investments in people are cheaper than investments in technology (Weber, Alcaro, and Ciotti, 2001).
- Workforce development enhances productivity and innovation in the organization.
- Culture governs the behavior of people (Corriss, 2010).
- Culture is developed and strengthened over time (Corriss, 2010).
- A strong cybersecurity or information assurance culture addresses a major source of breaches in organizations (Probst, et al., 2010).

Key Components of Cybersecurity Governance

- Values – the organization must adopt a set of values.
- Recruitment – the organization must recruit and retain people who reflect the organizational values.
- Policies – all legal, regulatory and organizational requirements must be reflected in enforceable policies.
- Engagement and innovation – all members of the organization must be engaged into the mission of the organization and actively work towards improving the areas they work in.
- Management involvement at all layers – organizational values, practices, policies and reinforcement must be supported by management at all layers of the organization.
- Transparency – before we can fix flaws, we have to admit to our people that these flaws exist.
- Monitoring – we need to monitor and discuss what is happening in the organization through the monitoring of behavior and results.
- Enforcement – there must be good balance between positive rewards and negative consequences for people.

- Non-disclosure contracts – everyone must agree to appropriate non-disclosure clauses which protect organizations – usually for perpetuity.
- Organization – the organizational structure must facilitate accountability and reflect clear lines of authority and must facilitate communication and collaboration throughout the organization.
- Accountability – who is responsible for what must be clearly identified and appropriate authority must accompany accountability.

Key Constituents for Cybersecurity Governance

Successful cybersecurity governance requires the active engagement of several key constituents and an organization must have a strategy to engage these critical stakeholders in its cybersecurity and business risk management strategy:

- Board – risks and strategy should be explained in business terms and how negative risks threaten the mission and how positive risks create opportunities to further the mission.
- Executive team – must engage in strategic collaboration.
- Legal and Risk Officers – must maintain a pulse on the legal and regulatory landscape and translate those into organizational requirements and develop appropriate impact analyses of all risks on a continuous basis.
- Human resources – develop recruiting, onboarding, training, and human resources development strategy around the values of the organization while ensuring that compensation and retention practices reflect fairness, market reality and the values of the organization.
- Contracts management – must update contract terms and conditions and establish appropriate contractual remedies for non-performance, damages for security breaches, appropriate handling of risk and personnel management. Simple service level agreement contracts are no longer sufficient.
- Middle management – must translate the mission, values, and policies into work and operational practices and procedures and continuously monitor their adherence.
- Organizational workers – adopt organizational mission and values in their work and develop and practice a cybersecurity culture.
- Regulatory/Legislative bodies – provide legal and policy frameworks which actually enhance cybersecurity without

becoming an unnecessary and expensive compliance burden without actually improving cybersecurity.

- Public – incorporate cybersecurity practices in work and personal lives, speak with their wallets and voices. Reward organizations which maintain better cybersecurity and penalize organizations which are negligent and callous with information. Ask simple questions such as, "Is my information maintained in an encrypted manner?" "What protections do you have in place to ensure that my personal information I am trusting you with will be protected.?" "Will you be selling my confidential information to others?"

Requirements for Success

- **Linkage and support from key constituents** – organizations must develop structures and processes to link with their key constituents and have a dialogue with them on a regular basis. Organizations must educate and provide transparency about their cybersecurity practices to their constituents and gain an acceptance of these practices.

- **Partnership and cooperation from user base** – organizations must gain cooperation from their information user base through representative policy development, widespread engagement in cybersecurity enhancements and innovation (Brown, 2005). The user base must also be engaged in oversight and vigilance – 1000 eyes are better than one.

Cybersecurity or Information Assurance Champions

In order to engage all members of the organization, cybersecurity or information assurance champions should be established in every work/stakeholder unit of the organization. These champions will help implement, maintain, and improve a successful cybersecurity culture. Their primary role will be to serve as liaison between the work/stakeholder group and the enterprise governance organization.

They will help to ensure that members of their work/stakeholder group are aware of the policies and requirements and can also help to surface concerns and proposed changes. They will also help to ensure that new members in their respective workgroups are informed and aware of the cybersecurity practices and their own roles and responsibilities in maintaining and improving the environment.

Factors that Determine Successful Cybersecurity Governance

- Organizational level for cybersecurity governance – the higher the level at which cybersecurity governance begins, the more likely it is to succeed (White 2009).
- CIO role and reporting level – organizations which treat CIOs as technical managers will fail to develop appropriate cybersecurity strategies (John, 2011; Moghadassi & Sheikhtaheri, 2010). Instead CIOs must be business minded executives who understand how to tie IT and cybersecurity to the mission. These executives must report to the highest levels of the organization for appropriate empowerment and influence on the organizational strategy.
- Executive management engagement -- without top level executive engagement, cybersecurity governance will fail (Adelman & Stokes, 2012; Brady, 2010; Schlienger & Teufel, 2003). An organization may have excellent technology and policies but uneven and inappropriate implementation, acceptance and enforcement.
- Benevolent management – when management takes care of workers, workers take care of the organization (Johnson & Warkentin, 2008). This is a simple human phenomenon.
- Employee empowerment – when people feel they can make a difference they will (Johnson & Warkentin, 2008). When organizations fail to engage and empower the entire workforce into the strategy the workforce is apathetic to the organization.
- Policy enforcement – people have to have a sense that policies have teeth or they will not follow them (Ross, et al., 2009). Management themselves need to adhere to the policies and establish positive and negative rewards to guide behavior.
- Monitoring – if people believe that their behavior is being monitored, chances are higher that they will exhibit desired behavior (Li & Shaw, 2008).
- Information security culture – information security culture is strongly associated with information security compliance behavior (Brady, 2010, Corriss, 2010; Hasib, 2013).

Practical Steps to Enterprise Cybersecurity Governance

The following are some key practical steps to an enterprise cybersecurity governance strategy:

- Identify values for organization and obtain buy in from the highest levels of the organization.

- Ensure that information security and privacy are components of these values.
- Identify the governance organization.
- Develop policies through a participative process.
- Develop the roll out, reinforcement, monitoring and enforcement of values and policies.
- Develop feedback mechanism for ideas and innovation.
- Develop a rewards and retribution structure.

The Positive Impact of Cybersecurity Governance

One of the key benefits of a widespread engagement of an organization's workers into a cybersecurity governance strategy is the dramatic rise in worker productivity and innovation. Technical proficiency of workers in professional and personal lives also rises. This automatically increases the courage to innovate and leads to a virtuous cycle of continuous improvement and risk reduction.

Risk Management and Compliance

Risk management and compliance strategy has to go hand in hand with an effective enterprise governance strategy. The following ten risk management and compliance areas should be addressed by any organization:

- System and Data Classification
- Security Controls
- Access Management
- Secure Infrastructure and Cloud Computing
- Data Encryption
- Audit Trails
- Continuity of Operations and Disaster Recovery
- Compliance Oversight
- Privacy
- Non-disclosure agreements

1. *System and Data Classification*

   All systems and data should be classified in accordance with the level of data protection required. Categories of High Risk, Moderate Risk, and Low Risk can be used.

   High Risk Data

   Systems and data which contain Protected Health Information (PHI) and Personally Identifiable Information (PII) are governed by several laws and should be classified as High Risk. Federal Tax Information (FTI) should also be classified as High Risk. Federal and military data systems have their own classification systems.

   Moderate Risk Data

   Data which do not contain PHI, PII, or FTI but contain sensitive, confidential, or proprietary information should be treated as moderate risk data.

Low Risk Data

All remaining data should be considered low risk.

2. *Security Controls*
   A multi-layered security control architecture should be used. A balanced framework of three types of controls should be used: technology, policy and procedures, and people management.

3. *Access Management*
   All personnel granted access to systems and data should have their identity, need to have access, duration for access, level of access (administer system, read, write, modify, delete), and training for appropriate use of access, reviewed and approved in writing by authorized people initially as well as on an ongoing basis. Access should be granted strictly according what is required to perform the job function. Access should be reviewed and revoked or modified whenever the job function changes. Documentation on all access approvers and the people to whom access has been provided should be maintained and reviewed for accuracy on a regular basis.

4. *Secure Infrastructure and Cloud Computing*
   The infrastructure used to provide services should use a layered security architecture with physical and logical segmentation of users and systems depending on risk. Such a risk based approach should be used by any cloud computing vendors in any cloud computing environment used by the organization.

5. *Data Encryption*
   All protected data at rest and in motion should be encrypted using appropriate technology. All organizational workers should be required to use appropriate encryption technology to protect laptops, tablets, thumb drives and other devices which could be easily lost, misplaced, or stolen.

6. *Audit Trails*
   All access to systems and data as well as changes to the systems and data should be logged and available for auditing purposes. System administrators should have no access to modify or delete these logs. These logs and audit trails should be reviewed periodically and systematically by an independent third-party.

7. *Continuity of Operations and Disaster Recovery*
   A disaster recovery plan, which includes a continuity of operations plan, should be developed and maintained. This plan should be reviewed and approved by management and tested for accuracy and compliance at least annually. These approvals and tests should be documented and the results should be shared publicly.

8. *Compliance Oversight*
   An independent verification and validation service should be used to provide compliance oversight. This service will provide the executives of the organization with periodic reports, analysis of the risk levels and compliance gaps, recommendation of remediation steps, and track the appropriate disposition of these risks.

9. *Privacy*
   All appropriate privacy policies relevant to the industry of the organization should be incorporated into the policy and compliance framework of the organization.

10. *Non-disclosure agreements*
   All personnel associated with the organization should be required to acknowledge that they have read and understood the data protection policies and sign non-disclosure agreements with a perpetual obligation to protect the information.

The Dramatic Change in the Role of the CIO

Once upon a time, information technology was used solely for payroll, accounting, finance, and human resources functions of an organization. IT involved writing code and performing compute functions. This is how the original concept of IT managers reporting to the Chief Financial Officer (CFO) or the VP of Administration and Finance initiated. I was among those early managers who started out my career in such an environment.

However, advent of the network and the internet changed everything. Today IT is hardly about computing or writing code. Information technology today is about growing the business, marketing, relationship management, communications, recruiting, intellectual capital, and most importantly -- business differentiation. This new environment has made IT a revenue engine and a mission critical function. The Chief Information Officer (CIO) is now the most important partner for the Chief Executive Officer (CEO).

Visionary CEOs who recognized and embraced this change, reaped amazing benefits from this great partnership – and so did their organizations and clients. Organizations such as universities were able to expand their markets globally. Teams could collaborate globally, and access to knowledge became universal and inexpensive. Work patterns changed. People no longer went to work during a particular time – rather they worked from wherever they pleased and whenever they pleased.

As technology began to drive the mission of organizations, specially during the last 20 years, the role of the Chief Information Officer began to evolve from an operational role to a strategic role. At the same time, the role went from the computer room to the board room. Almost all projects today have become IT projects; and they need to be run by proven IT executives in order to ensure success. Finally, an enhanced focus on cybersecurity has become integral to the role of the Chief Information Officer.

At first glance, due to the business purpose, many projects may appear to be healthcare projects or billing projects or marketing projects or education projects. In the past, these projects may been run successfully by business executives with no IT backgrounds. Today, given their complex and precise technology and cybersecurity requirements, they require IT project management discipline and proven IT executives to lead them. While business executives may decide what should be done, IT executives must decide how it should be done.

Cloud computing and the need to restrain infrastructure costs have added another major complexity – the need to manage contracts and their risks. We also need plans for disengagements in the event a cloud service provider relationship turns sour – or the cloud service provider goes out of business, or gets acquired. These provisions need to be reflected in the contracts. These changes require a new breed of CIOs. However, I see a high degree of inconsistent implementation in the business environment and the CIO role continues to be widely misunderstood.

In some organizations, the CIO is part of the Chief Executive Officer's cabinet. This person is fully informed and engaged in the business strategy. Information technology in these organizations is viewed as a strategic asset – something that moves the organization forward. In other organizations, the CIO may report to the Chief Financial Officer or some other role lower down in the organization. Information technology in these organizations is viewed as a cost center, and technology decisions are rarely strategic in nature.

Organizations that understand the CIO role -- and the skills required to fulfill it -- establish appropriate reporting structures and focus their recruiting efforts on finding business-minded IT leaders with strong skills in communications and relationship building. Organizations that do not understand the role may simply retitle a director or manager of information technology without any change in empowerment, reporting relationships, or required skills.

A CIO has to invest in the future and spend a significant amount of resources on research and development, innovation, problem avoidance, and risk management. An organization where the CFO has veto power over the CIO will frequently forgo many strategic technology and cybersecurity investments. When the problems surface, it is too late!

Multiple years of technology or cybersecurity stagnation cannot be fixed in an instant. Organizational reputation damage cannot be undone. Sadly, even though the CFO is in charge, the CIO will bear the consequences when problems happen. Empirical examples of this phenomenon is quite common in both public and private sectors and I have personally experienced them.

Another part of the problem is that many institutional leaders still view the CIO role as a technical one. During a dinner event after a conference, I was seated next to the president of an organization. I asked him, "Do you have a CIO in your organization?" Perkily he said with a big smile, "Yes, I do." I followed up with, "So your CIO attends your cabinet meetings and is a member of your institutional strategy team?" His expression told me that he was visibly taken aback by this question.

"No, I do not want a technical person in my cabinet," he said rather emphatically, as though wondering why I would even ask this question. In the conversation that followed, we were worlds apart. I tried to convince him that a CIO is not a technical person but a business person who understands how technology fits into the business strategy. He tried to convince me that the CIO's job was to "keep things running."

Clearly, this was another example of an organization that had simply retitled a director of IT position and was calling it a CIO -- perhaps following a perceived trend without understanding what the role truly entails -- just so he could say, "Me too." During the conversation, it also became clear that this organization would stagnate under this President. Until the President changed, this organization's future was bleak. Blaming the CIO for cybersecurity problems in such an organization is morally wrong.

Granted there are instances where someone with the CIO title/role is not sufficiently engaged in learning the business or attempting to align the technology strategy with the business mission. Many CIOs have also failed to incorporate cybersecurity into their strategy. Sometimes, they are too enamored with implementing the latest technology, or unable to tie an acquisition, idea or proposal to the business mission.

I have seen CIOs of large institutions solely focused on a vendor driven perennial technology refresh cycle – something that may justifiably earn IT the reputation of being a money pit. Some of these CIOs even mocked others for not having the latest and greatest in what they had. These CIOs do not understand that each investment must have a clear payoff in furthering the mission of the organization and must address organizational priorities or serve to distinguish the institution somehow. A refresh cycle should be tied to a critical project that the organization needs. Many upgrades are completely unnecessary and simply serve as a vendor revenue stream.

Some CIOs may have a language barrier. I have frequently heard the complaint, "My president does not understand technology." We cannot expect the CEO of an organization to understand technology. However, most CEOs have business goals they wish to achieve, and as long as we are focused on those goals and working to tie the technology and cybersecurity strategy to the mission, most CEOs will listen. The conversation must be about business goals, creating value, moving forward, competitive edge or distinction for the organization -- not about technology.

Seven Essential Functions of a CIO

What then are the functions of a CIO? A couple of years ago, when the security breach at LinkedIn occurred, I was perturbed to learn that they had neither a CIO nor a Chief Information Security Officer (CISO). During the more recent breach at Target, I was equally surprised to learn Target did not have a CISO either. While Target had a CIO, I did not observe any cybersecurity credentials in this role. The TV and public appearances by the CFO convinced me that the CFO was really in charge – yet the CIO had to take the fall. Interestingly, it appeared that the CEO also took the fall.

LinkedIn executives explained that their VP of Engineering and VP of Operations were performing CIO and CISO functions. Certainly, in terms of personal qualifications, these executives may have the skills to perform the CIO role. However, CIOs have a much wider perspective of the organization compared to the perspective of a single-functional unit executive. The CIO role spans seven key functions as shown in the picture below:

The Seven Essential Functions of a CIO

In 2010, while presenting the role of the CIO at a conference, I developed this simple graphical model to illustrate these functions, to facilitate discussions, and to explain my role as a CIO to others. It is very important to note that many of these functions are new and have never been part of the job role of a typical Director or Manager of Information Technology.

Although the goals of confidentiality, integrity, and availability have been around for a long time, as a holistic discipline or even a word, cybersecurity is barely ten years old! Yet it is now an integral part of a CIO's role. Building and maintaining relationships hardly mattered in the past – the primary role was operational -- to "keep things running."

During a highly interactive session at Educause (Hasib, Swartz, & Finn, 2011), we had to explain the role of the CIO to about 100 current and aspiring CIOs and people who worked for them. Before we presented the graphical model, we asked the audience to identify all the functions of a CIO they could think of; more than 20 functions were identified. Then we revealed the model. Everyone agreed that all 20 functions identified by the audience could neatly fit into seven key functions:

1. Strategic Planning
2. Building and Maintaining Relationships
3. Cybersecurity
4. Reliability and Quality
5. Projects and Services
6. Promoting the Organization
7. Team Building

It became very clear to everyone that other IT roles, such as VP of engineering, VP of operations, or even a director of IT, do not encompass all seven essential CIO functions. While many of these functions can be successfully delegated, a CIO must personally focus on team building, relationships, and promoting the organization – while maintaining a pulse on the other functional areas.

Team building is now central to the role of the CIO. Success will quickly become elusive if this critical function is delegated or abdicated. Though all CIOs are responsible for all seven functions, most will need to share responsibility with key deputies and other leaders who form the CIO's core leadership team.

For example, due to the increasing complexity and need for strategic focus on cybersecurity, most organizations will need separate information security and/or information privacy officers. In some cases, these designated positions are required by law. However, due to differing skill requirements, it is important to carefully select the right leader for each area. It is equally important to ensure that all leaders are functioning as a cohesive team and are collaboratively working for each other's success and the overall success of the organization.

Building and managing relationships, both within and outside the organization, is critical for a CIO in order to recognize priorities, trends, emerging problems, and opportunities. Discussions and engagement with industry peers will help to validate and fine-tune strategies and ensure continuous learning. Relationships are also essential in promoting the organization.

Promoting the organization through continuous analysis and discussion of the economic impact of IT on the rest of the organization connects the IT function to its stakeholders in a meaningful way. It ties the success of programs and initiatives to the success of IT. It promotes effective use of IT services and ensures an understanding of how IT strategy fulfills the mission of the organization.

For these three areas, skillful communications and strong interpersonal skills are critical assets for a CIO. While a strong technical and/or cybersecurity background may help, success is usually determined by a CIO's ability to listen, communicate, collaborate, build relations, and collaboratively develop a shared vision.

Most of a CIO's strategic communications must be in plain business language. For example, a cybersecurity strategy is usually best explained in terms of the value of business risks mitigated, financial loss avoided, or additional revenue generated rather than in opaque technical terms such as "advanced persistent threats" or "phishing."

To underscore an essential point: The CIO role is best performed at the highest executive levels of the organization – in the C-suite -- above the engineering or operations level.

The Error of Not Having a CIO

So what can happen if an organization does not have a CIO? Is the position so vital? Why happens when organizations keep this position vacant for years at a time – sometimes to save money because a CEO or a CFO thinks it is the right thing to do? Let me relate a true story I observed.

I was talking to the CEO of a major urban hospital which had never had a CIO and decided to look for one in 2013. Despite the Health Information Technology for Economic and Clinical Health (HITECH) Act of 2009, this CEO continued his institution's policy of not hiring a CIO or CISO. He had hired a respected consulting company to analyze his technology environment and they had informed him that his organization was seriously short staffed in the technology area.

Like many others, he took a wait-and-see attitude, even though HITECH strengthened the enforcement of healthcare security and privacy laws, and provided financial incentives for healthcare organizations to adopt electronic health records and information security. In 2010, as part of the federal government's Meaningful Use program, while other organizations were getting a portion of billions of dollars in federal incentive money to implement health information technology (HIT), this CEO did nothing -- until someone mentioned that penalties loomed for non-compliance.

After a three-year delay, the CEO finally decided to hire a CIO. Correctly, he opted to have the CIO report to him as a member of the cabinet; clearly he wanted someone with a strategic vision. The CEO's requirements were stringent, and he was emphatic about his needs.

"I want someone who has already implemented Meaningful Use somewhere. We need to implement it very quickly here," he said.

His IT department, board of directors, and human resource staff all echoed the same sentiment:

"Since Meaningful Use is very new, few people have actual experience with it. These CIOs are in high demand, there are very few of them to go around, and they are very expensive. You really do not need to make this a hiring criterion. Implementing Meaningful Use should be similar to any IT project; just look for a track record of successful program or project management. Experience at organizational adoption of technology will be important. Implementation is one thing. Getting everyone to use it and navigating through the associated security and privacy compliance will also be important. Our hospital should also hire a chief information security officer."

"Our budget is limited right now," the CEO retorted.

"You will also need to hire a project manager or a senior systems engineer to help with the implementation," his advisors said.

"Actually, I am looking for a CIO who is very hands-on, someone who can implement and upgrade the software as well," replied the CEO, pensively.

"But the CIO is not an operational role. Your CIO will need to follow everything that's going on in the industry and ensure that what happened to this organization in the past does not happen again. If the person has operational duties too, he or she will not be successful in *either* role. There is no good way to divide these roles. A true CIO would not be happy with an operational role," the increasingly frustrated advisory group noted.

"In our organization, everyone, including me, has an operational role. I get into contract negotiations and solve many problems," the CEO said earnestly.

This type of conversation occurs in many organizations. I find it amazing they continue even today when technology drives everything and IT strategy is equivalent to organizational strategy in any business, government, or educational organization. Quality CIOs know more about how an organization functions than any other C-level executive. They cannot focus on the big picture if they're bogged down in operational details. In order to keep moving forward organizations must leverage the resources of a CIO.

Why CFOs Should Not Control IT Strategy

Though many organizations may think organizational structure does not matter, it matters greatly. Most of us would balk at riding an airplane being driven by a bus driver – unless the bus driver actually had established credentials to fly the airplane! So why would we use our Chief Financial Officer to drive our IT strategy?

The other day I read an article that talked about a chief marketing officer (CMO) who spent more on IT than the CIO did. Upon reading further, I learned that departments buy what they want and the CIO must support these technologies. What?! That is not the role of a CIO. In fact, that sounds very much like an operational role rather than a strategic one. In other words, this is another company where a director of IT has the title of CIO, but no empowerment or strategic role.

In the government sector, the problem appears to be even worse. Despite spending incredible amounts on IT, agencies rarely reap the benefits, because spending may be in the wrong hands with no strategy behind it. In many government organizations CIOs continue to report to CFO-type executives. The IT budget remains in the hands of these CFO-like people or in the hands of various program heads, resulting in fragmented spending. Every 12 months, agencies make a final splurge at fiscal year-end to ensure no money remains on the table – with a large chunk spent on unnecessary and even obsolete technology.

You would not believe how many times I have heard government agency heads tell their people: "Make sure no money is left in any account. We do not want to return any money." The easiest way to spend money is to buy computers and laptops -- whether you need them or not. What an incredible way to waste taxpayer money.

When CIOs report to CFOs, these financial executives frequently assume that they have the expertise to make IT decisions. After all, managing information technology was a course in their MBA studies!

Consider this recent example: Program leaders wanted tablets for their light weight, mobility, language support, ease of use, and cost. The CIO was supportive of the concept -- it was certainly the right strategic direction --

but the agency would need to invest in some training and mobile-device-management software. The CFO ruled: "We do not know how to support tablets. Laptops are mobile devices. Buy laptops." So the agency continued to buy laptops for $2,000 each when tablets that cost less than $500 would have done the job better. Worse, the agency wasted an opportunity to move forward.

In the mid 1980s, I walked into an organization where the entire IT department had just been fired by the CFO (VP of Administration and Finance). I learned that the organization had purchased a $5.5 million dollar mainframe which never worked and parts of it were tucked away in some closet. Like me, another young IT professional had also been hired and we were asked to "make this mainframe work."

After researching the issue and after assessing why they had purchased the mainframe, we both realized several things:

1. The mainframe was obsolete at the time of purchase and the vendor gave them a major discount – so the CFO thought he was saving money.
2. Trying to make the mainframe work would require another $2 million which the CFO had budgeted for but would require us to hire programmers and develop custom software – a highly risky and time consuming venture.
3. Even if we succeeded, the mainframe would only do payroll, accounting, and student records and would do nothing for office automation or research analysis which the institution needed.
4. The strategy would be wrong for the time. A local area network spanning the three buildings using mostly off the shelf software (which could be customized) would allow all business functions that the institution needed: accounting, finance, payroll, student records, office automation, research support using statistical software and electronic mail.
5. Our alternate strategy would cost about one-tenth of the original plan and increase the productivity of the entire organization. We could transform the organization and prepare it for the future and get everyone excited about the new world.
6. We would realize additional cost savings by retiring typewriters, key punch machines, green and orange dumb terminals, and many other things.
7. We could deploy the technology in a planned and phased way to allow the people in the organization to absorb the technology incrementally.

Our main problem was convincing the CFO who had made this huge public investment of this alternate vision. As we started to share our ideas, these ideas started to gain traction with the faculty and the academic side of the institution. Even the administrative and accounting staff loved the idea of office automation, shared files and printers on the network and instant communication through e-mail. The President and all the other leaders of the institution accepted our vision and gave us the money to implement.

Unfortunately, even though we had saved the institution millions of dollars, increased the productivity of the faculty and staff and moved the organization forward by decades, since IT continued to report to the CFO, and since we had just gone against the vision of the CFO, life for us became miserable. We were not even interviewed for the newly created Director of Computing position. We were told, "You are too young."

Yes, it was my cue that it was time to move on and I am really glad things turned out this way because I may never have experienced some of the later adventures of my career. I felt the warmth and gratitude of the people we had served when 400 of the institution's 500 people including the institution's President and all executive leaders attended my farewell reception and gave me their warmest hugs and their sincere best wishes.

This lack of empowerment, or ability to oversee an organization's strategy often means great CIOs won't stick around in organizations where they are probably needed most – because CFOs are running the IT in these organizations. CIOs move around a lot, with about 12 to 18 months usually being the breaking point. Another article cited a "wise sage" who questioned the viability of the CIO, and claimed that organizations (and in particular some CFOs) already are beginning to realize they can do without this top-level professional.

Do these people have their heads in the sand? In an era when IT drives every aspect of every business; when cybersecurity is the highest priority problem in every organization; when IT is becoming more complex; when appropriate sourcing of services is a critical decision; when planning for disasters is mandatory; when negotiating and managing the risks of highly detailed IT service contracts is standard operating procedure; and when cybersecurity strategy could mean the difference between an organization's survival or demise, why do some pundits actually predict the obsolescence of the CIO role? I predict a transformation of more CISOs into CIO roles and more CIOs into CEO roles. The traditional trend of CFOs moving to

CEO positions is another anachronism that must change for organizations to move forward through a technology and cybersecurity powered strategy.

In all my years interacting with CFOs, I have not met one who actually understood IT -- not that I expected them to. Yet we continue to see ads seeking a strategic CIO who will report to the VP of Administration and Finance or the CFO. Sometimes ads are slightly better: CIOs report to the Chief Operating Officer. Those conducting the recruitment will sagely say: "The CIO will have complete empowerment and access to all cabinet members and the president." However, these organizations appear to lack an understanding of the role of the CIO *and* the CFO.

Sometimes organizations are so entrenched in an organizational structure that they fail to recognize the changes around them. The following story illustrates one of the funniest reasons I have ever heard.

I met a hospital CIO at a conference who had been in an organization for nearly 30 years. The CFO and the President had been in the organization about the same length of time. It was time for the CFO to retire. So the CIO went to the President and asked for a reporting change to the President. He argued that it was only fair and that the organization would have trouble recruiting for his position when the CIO himself retired.

The President replied, "Now you know you have access to me anytime. You know that we are promoting the Deputy CFO to the CFO position. If I make this change now, what will the new CFO think? He will think I made the change because I thought he could not run IT. We can't have that." It was difficult to argue with such logic.

Although the CIO hated the situation, he could not leave because he was close to retirement himself as was the President. Even then if the CFO rose to the rank of President, with internal promotions this vicious cycle may continue for a long while – until some major catastrophe strikes.

VPs of Administration and Finance represent the interests of that business vertical. They are also strongly partial to the systems used by that business vertical. For example, within a medical university, they cannot be expected to also represent marketing; advancement; communications; business development; client relations; disease control; provost; faculty; student life; or other departments. Think about your enterprise: How can the person overseeing finance be impartial or well-informed across all your departments?

Under many organizations' reporting structures, the CIO is expected to develop relationships with these other business verticals, but since they report to the CFO they are excluded from the very cabinet meetings where leaders congregate. Even when CIOs are invited, they are not considered of equal rank -- because they are not. Everyone views the CFO as the final authority for IT decisions, leading to some serious problems.

In these organizations, finance drives strategy instead of strategy driving finance. IT is seen as a cost center and there is a perennial pressure to cut costs and reduce expenditures -- often at the detriment of strategy. Cybersecurity may be non-existent in these organizations. Setting appropriate salaries for CIOs and people reporting to the CIOs becomes impossible.

Take those many CFO-reporting organizations looking to hire chief information security officers. Since the CIO's salary structure is low, CISO salaries are lower. When the CIO discusses setting an appropriate salary, no amount of market data will overcome the CFO's retort of: "This is what we can afford" -- without understanding the risks involved in hiring the wrong person for the job due to an arbitrary, non-market based salary. I have seen months-long CISO hiring processes break down at the final moment because of an arbitrary salary level. I have even asked human resources: "Does your market analysis show this is the right compensation level?" The answer, invariably, is, "No, but this is what we can afford."

In these organizations, CIO salaries can be $50,000 to $100,000 less than the CFO's pay. This makes no sense when the CIO is expected to work with all executives as well as the president and contribute to the organization's strategy. Paying inadequately prevents you from hiring the best-suited, most experienced CIO, potentially creating a disaster waiting to happen for both the executive and the organization.

After all, although the CFO will make the ultimate decision on the IT strategy, the CIO will remain responsible for it -- and all consequences of these decisions will rest upon the CIO. I have witnessed countless examples of these failed CIO experiments.

In the organization's case, the appropriate IT and cybersecurity strategy will not be implemented. The organization is likely to fall far behind in technology investments and upgrades.

Personnel will be hard to retain due to the artificially depressed salary structure. The CIO will most likely be relegated to an operational and maintenance role -- and may find this to be the only way to maintain sanity. Modern organizations should carefully avoid this very dangerous situation.

The CISO's Role in the Organization

The complexity and the highly operational skills needed to be successful has also resulted in the critical role of the Chief Information Security Officer. The primary role of this executive is to focus on developing and executing the strategy for maximizing confidentiality, integrity, and availability of technology and systems as a key partner for a CIO. Initially the role was not as complex. So a CIO could do this role effectively.

What then is the relationship between a CIO and a CISO? We have seen that the CIO's role encompasses seven areas shown in the earlier graphic which is repeated below for convenience. Several of these areas have strong operational components. The CIO's role leans heavily on the strategic side - - ensuring the future, while the CISO's role leans heavily on the operational side. Both roles have a high degree of overlap and it is essential that the CIO and CISO have a strong mutually supportive working relationship.

The Seven Essential Functions of a CIO

The circles toward the top and upper left lean on the strategic side, and the CIO must concentrate on those personally. The circles toward the right and bottom lean on the operational side, which the CIO should delegate to other leaders with specialized skills. Someone with the right skill set, an understanding of the CIO's role, and a strong cybersecurity/information assurance background would be an ideal fit as a deputy CIO/CISO overseeing all of these operational roles. The CISO's role includes strategic components but it is much more focused on operational tasks and has continuous operational engagement with all aspects of an organization.

The CIO and the CISO should be collaborative and constructive partners. They must have an open relationship. Constructive debates, and continuous professional growth should be encouraged and accepted. All operational unit heads should report to the deputy CIO/CISO (in at least a matrix format), because cybersecurity must be ingrained into every operational unit.

The deputy CIO/CISO must work collaboratively with all units to ensure a culture of cybersecurity is infused into every staff member. This will substantially relieve the CIO from operational duties. However, the CIO and CISO should cover for each other during absences.

A good CISO will need a solid technical background, a history of continuous learning, and a demonstrated ability to talk to network engineers, server engineers, application programmers, lawyers, risk managers, human resources, and others at an operational level. This individual should collaboratively examine the organization and lead the development of a cybersecurity governance framework. Ideally the person should be comfortable in both CIO and CISO roles.

Without an understanding of both roles, it will be difficult for either the CIO or the CISO to succeed. The work relationship among all IT department leaders must be grounded on complete trust and collaboration. Ideas and policies should belong to the entire team, not just one person. Everyone must support the final decision, and infighting should be unacceptable.

Recruiting CIOs and CISOs

Organizations must ensure that their Chief Information Officer position has the right reporting relationship, fair market compensation and appropriate authority to be effective in the position. Hiring the wrong candidate due to artificial organizational and financial barriers will cost organizations a lot more in the long run.

In mid 2013, I saw an ad for a Chief Information Technology Officer with a salary range of $73K-$92K for a community college in Maryland with about 10,000 students. During the previous President's term and partially during the current President's term, the CIO position at this institution was a Vice President position reporting directly to the President. The salary range at that time was about $10K higher.

Since the position reported to the President, it was certainly defined as a strategic position requiring someone with business and communications skills and a strong understanding of the mission of the organization – someone who could be a partner for the President – someone who could translate the President's vision into a technology strategy. The problem is that at the salary level defined, it was impossible to find a CIO with the appropriate skills.

With the new ad, it appears they decided to save an additional $10K by eliminating a VP position and having the CIO report to the VP for Finance and Operations – in effect they will now have their CFO determine their IT strategy. Unfortunately, at this range and reporting relationship, they have no chance of finding someone qualified. To make matters worse, the institution does not have a Chief Information Security Officer and according to the ad, expects the CIO to perform in a dual role.

Unfortunately the people making these organizational hiring decisions do not understand IT or the appropriate hiring ranges for these positions and are creating dangerous conditions for the institution.

Job Summary			
Chief Information Technology Officer			POSTED: May 20
Job Code: 140-2013			
Salary:	$ 73,484.00 - 91,855.00	Location:	Bel Air, Maryland
Employer:	Harford Community College	Type:	Full Time - Experienced
Categories:	Senior/Mid-Level Management, Technical (Programmer, Developer, Analyst)	Required Education:	Masters

Apply For This Job   Email Job   Save Job

Job Description

HCC is seeking an experienced Information Technology professional to provide vision and leadership for developing and implementing information systems and technology initiatives. The Chief Information Technology Officer is responsible for directing, planning, implementing, upgrading, and supporting enterprise systems and technology, including all related equipment and tools, in support of the academic and administrative needs of the College.

The CIO leads IT strategic and operational planning; is responsible for maintaining a secured information and technology infrastructure; manages enterprise-wide disaster recovery and business continuity plan; approves, prioritizes and oversees information technology projects, including hardware and software acquisitions and systems upgrades; ensures continuous delivery of network and telecommunication services; supervises recruitment, development, retention, and organization of all IT staff in accordance with College policies, and performs other duties as assigned by the supervisor.

This is an exempt, administrator position reporting to the Vice President for Finance and Operations.

Requirements

A master's degree in Computer Science, Information Systems, Information Technology, Computer Engineering, or Business Administration and five to seven years experience leading, managing, and/or directing a small to medium sized IT organization are required. Applicants must have experience in strategic planning and execution; substantial experience in data processing, information systems, networking and computing, including disaster recovery; supervisory experience; and the ability to manage budgets.

Visit our Web site at http://www.harford.edu/HR/jobs.asp to view job details and apply online. Online application must include a cover letter and resume. For best consideration apply by June 9, 2013.

HCC is a smoke/tobacco-free campus. HCC is an AA/EEO/ADA employer committed to diversity in the college community.

The next ad at the State of Maryland Department of Labor, Licensing and Regulation for a Chief Information Security Officer with a salary range of $48K-$76K is also from 2013. This ad does not state where the position reports. However, I cannot imagine anyone qualified to be a CISO in Maryland accepting a position at this salary range.

STATE OF MARYLAND JOB OPENINGS

COMPUTER NETWORK SPECIALIST LEAD

Powered by Job

Chief Information Security Officer

Recruitment #13-004503-001

DATE OPENED	4/15/2013 11:30:00 AM
FILING DEADLINE	4/29/2013 11:59:00 PM
SALARY	$47,495.00 - $76,220.00/year
EMPLOYMENT TYPE	Full-Time
HR ANALYST	Elaine Grimes
WORK LOCATION	Baltimore City

Go Back   Click HERE to view benefits

INTRODUCTION

This is a position specific recruitment for the Department of Labor, Licensing and Regulation. This recruitment will be used to fill this position/function only. The resulting eligible list will be maintained for one year. Persons interested in future vacancies within this classification must re-apply.

GRADE

18

LOCATION OF POSITION

Baltimore City, Maryland

MAIN PURPOSE OF JOB

This position plans, implements, and monitors security and Continuity of Operations Planning (COOP) disaster recovery measures for the protection of computer networks and information within DLLR.

The following ad offers a healthy contrast. It is clearly an ad for a strategic CIO role reporting to the CEO who will be expected to use technology to implement the organizational vision. This organization understands the CIO role and the CEO is clearly looking for a partner and a key member of the cabinet.

Description

The CIO reports to the CEO and is responsible for defining, leading, and executing on DTI's vision for Information Technology.

The Chief Information Officer's role is to provide vision and leadership for developing and implementing information technology initiatives across all business units. The Chief Information Officer will direct the planning and implementation of enterprise IT systems in support of business operations in order to improve cost effectiveness, service quality, and business development. This individual is responsible for all aspects of the organization's information technology and systems, including multiple large datacenters.

DTI employ's a SAAS delivery model in providing technology-enabled legal services to its clients. The CIO will be accountable for the design, development, implementation of infrastructure associated with DTI's multiple 24x7x365 hosting data centers and network of 25 regional and local processing centers located around the US. .

Strategy & Planning

Participate in strategic and operational governance processes of the business organization as a member of the senior management team.
Lead IT strategic and operational planning to achieve business goals by fostering innovation, prioritizing IT initiatives, and coordinating the evaluation, deployment, and management of current and future IT systems and Development team across the organization.
Develop and maintain an appropriate IT organizational structure that supports the needs of the business.
Establish IT departmental goals, objectives, and operating procedures.
Identify opportunities for the appropriate and cost-effective investment of financial resources in IT systems and resources, including staffing, sourcing, purchasing, and in-house development.
Assess and communicate risks associated with IT investments to Senior management
Develop, track, and control the information technology annual operating and capital budgets.
Develop business case justifications and cost/benefit analyses for IT and Development spending and initiatives.
Direct development and execution of an enterprise-wide disaster recovery and business continuity plan.
Assess and make recommendations on the improvement or re-engineering of the IT organization.

The following ad for a statewide university system office is interesting as this model is common in many states where the system level CIO reports to the system level CFO – reducing the level of empowerment for the CIO and ensuring that finances and budgets will drive IT instead of strategy. Even though most system offices have academic officers – and education is the mission of the university systems, it is not clear why reporting to the CFO makes sense. Although I think the CIO should report to the system President or Chancellor, the next best alternative is for the CIO to report to the chief academic officer – not the finance and budget officer. The chances of the wrong person being hired is high. If the right person is obtained, the person will have difficulty building and maintaining relationships due to lack of empowerment and autonomy.

The following two ads offer another interesting CIO reporting relationship I have observed in higher education – to the Provost. This is a slightly better situation since the primary mission of this institution is education so the CIO can be a strong partner for the Provost who is likely to be focused on the mission. Note however that the ad states that the CIO will be required to also serve the needs of the administrative departments and will need to forge relationships with the Provost's peers – as well as the President.

If that is the case, why is the person reporting to the Provost? This reporting relationship will depress the salary of the CIO by one whole level. In addition, the CIO will have trouble gaining appropriate access to the leaders he/she needs to collaborate with. In addition he/she will lack the empowerment and authority needed to forge an appropriate strategy. At this institution, the Provost will be determining the IT strategy – resulting in a bias towards the academic systems – often at the detriment of administrative and other systems. It is not as bad as the CFO running IT for the institution, but this is not ideal either.

Chief Information Officer

Walsh University

The Chief Information Officer (CIO) guides the development and implementation of Walsh's information technology strategy and oversees the delivery of effective university technology services. The CIO leads the Division of Information Technology and is responsible for academic computing support, enterprise applications systems and services, networking and telecommunications, information security, data center operations, and user support, training and outreach.

The CIO builds and sustains effective partnerships and collaborations with academic and administrative departments, maintains a service oriented and agile IT organization, and a reliable and secure technology infrastructure. In consultation with university leadership and faculty, the CIO provides technologies and support services to enable teaching and learning, including the design for an innovative new learning center. The CIO leads the deployment of an upgraded wired and wireless network, improve the reliability and performance of core technologies, expand support for hybrid and in-person instruction and optimize the use of the Banner administrative system. The CIO and the IT organization partner with students, faculty and staff to identify and explore innovative ways to use technology to further the University's mission and goals in ways which balance and respect the institution's culture.

A direct report to the Provost, the CIO is an advocate for Walsh's total technology needs, facilitates IT governance, advises the cabinet on significant IT investments, and designs appropriate policies to manage technology and information security risk. The CIO leads the development and implementation of a technology sourcing strategy that leverages collaborations and corporate providers to optimize information technology services. He/she leads an IT organization that maintains high levels of performance and provides opportunities for IT professionals to increase their skills and contributions to the university.

e.edu/jobs/5452465

Chief Information Officer

Franklin Pierce University

 SHARE ☐ ☐ ☐ ... ☐ ☐ Email ☐ Print

Franklin Pierce University is undergoing exciting changes as we celebrate 50 years of outstanding leadership in education. We are an institution that is committed to liberal arts and sciences, and focuses on preparing students to be stewards and leaders of conscience who will make significant contributions to their professions and communities both locally and globally. Franklin Pierce invites expressions of interest for the integral position of Chief Information Officer.

The Chief Information Officer provides vision and leadership in the development and implementation of the university-wide information and educational technology programs and infrastructure in support of the University's mission and strategic goals. The CIO will support teaching, learning, scholarship, and project management operations, as well as engage students, staff, and faculty in the use of technology for the University's two organizational divisions: The College at Rindge and the College of Graduate and Professional Studies. The CIO reports to the University Provost/Vice President for Academic Affairs.

Confidential screening of applications and nominations will begin immediately and continue until the position is filled. However, for priority consideration, applications and nominations must be received by June 21, 2013.

As an Equal Opportunity Employer, we strongly encourage women and minorities to apply for our positions, and welcome enquiry from qualified applicants. For further information, please contact Janette Merideth in confidence at meridethj@franklinpierce.edu.

Applicants should send a detailed letter of application, a resume/CV, and contact details for three references to: Chief Information Officer Search, Franklin Pierce University, 40 University Drive, Rindge, NH 03461 or via email to jobs@franklinpierce.edu. EOE

The successful candidate will possess a master's degree in Information Technology or a similar discipline; a terminal degree is preferred. They will demonstrate progressive experience in senior level leadership in a business or academic environment and have innovative ideas about IT infrastructure. The successful candidate will demonstrate strong program planning, collaboration abilities and organizational skills and possess exceptional communication skills. It is understood

The next ad is for a CIO in healthcare. The position reports to the CEO and clearly requires the IT mission to be aligned with the organizational mission. The salary level and empowerment is expected to be appropriate. The expectation of an IT enabled innovation should be exciting for any CIO. This is definitely an ad for a real CIO.

Job Description

Direct the information and data strategy of the company and take a leadership role in the alignment of IT initiatives to the company's strategic objectives to create business value from Information Technology (IT) investments while leading the IT function to streamline processes, improve the quality of IT services, and pursue IT-enabled innovation.

Potential Career Path

Sr. Vice President of Information Technology – Chief Information Officer (CIO)

Reporting Structure

Reports directly to the HMM Chief Executive Officer.

Essential Job Functions

Strategic Planning and Implementation of Company's Information Technology Priorities

Set the IT mission and vision of the company and develop, execute, and direct the company'sstrategic and operational IT plans in terms of collecting, storing, and disseminating information.

Integrate IT services and solutions across different departments and functions while addressing each department's/function's unique requirements.

Collaborate with hotel partners to ensure the continuity and company-wide integration of all systems, applications, and data consistent with the company's IT mission.

Establish and direct the strategic and tactical goals, policies, and procedures ofthe IT function and ensure alignment of IT strategy with the company's overall business strategy.

Contrast that with the following ad – also in healthcare. This institution has an annual budget of about $10 billion and about 8000 employees. The CIO role is highly important because of technology driven strategic initiatives.

However, a key problem with this ad is the salary range. The reporting relationship to Operations is also a problem. It is possible that someone aspiring to be a CIO may be willing to accept the role as their first CIO job at the low salary range.

It is also likely that the focus for the position will be on operations rather than strategy. Hence, an operational person is most likely to be selected. The ad also stresses providing "technical assistance and advice" to the senior management – the ultimate decision makers. The CIO is clearly not among the organizational decision makers – most likely a key factor in the depressed salary structure and lack of empowerment. This is essentially a Director of IT position and not a CIO position. Since the CISO position in healthcare is becoming critical, if this organization wished to hire a CISO, the lower CIO salary level will result in an ever lower CISO salary level. Thus they will recruit the wrong people in both these critical positions..

Po

CHIEF INFORMATION OFFICER
PROGRAM MANAGER SENIOR IV
Recruitment #13-005485-002

DATE OPENED	3/21/2013 1:26:00 PM
FILING DEADLINE	4/4/2013 11:59:00 PM
SALARY	$79,798.00 - $128,258.00/year
EMPLOYMENT TYPE	Full-Time
HR ANALYST	Beth Reid
WORK LOCATION	Baltimore City

Go Back   Click HERE to view benefits

GRADE

26

LOCATION OF POSITION

Office of Information Technology (OIT), Baltimore, MD

Main Purpose Of Job

The incumbent within this position reports to the Deputy Secretary of Operations and serves as the Chief Information Officer for the Offi Information Technology (OIT) within the Department of Health and Mental Hygiene (DHMH). DHMH consists of a central headquarters loc Baltimore, Maryland and numerous field locations to include local health departments, mental health hospitals, developmental disability rehabilitation centers. OIT provides department-wide information technology planning, acquisition, policies and standards, local and wid computer networks, and the development, maintenance, and operations of information systems. The incumbent within this position mus vision, technical expertise, and IT business knowledge to see the future of technology and the determination to implement this vision an business goals under often changing and difficult circumstances. Additional skills the ideal candidate will posses includes a demonstrate proven leadership, high level judgment and decision making, management of financial resources, strategic and critical thinking, and com solving within an information technology structure.

Essential job functions the incumbent within this position will complete include providing technical assistance and advice to the Secretar Secretary's and senior management within DHMH, oversee the information management and data integrity for DHMH, provide project m oversight on a wide array of projects, including ones related to the implementation of the Affordable Care Act, direct the department-wi technology emergency management program, manage all information technology functions, and ensures the departments security and programs are established and maintained.

MINIMUM EDUCATION OR GENERAL REQUIREMENTS

A Bachelor's degree in an information technology, business, or management field and six years of information technology experience, fo which were at a management or supervisory level. Additional information technology experience will substitute on a year for year basis bachelor's degree. A related master's degree will also substitute for one year of the general experience.

SELECTION PROCESS

While the above ad was for a government agency, the following ad is for a private company in healthcare where the CIO will report to the CFO. Once again, it is difficult for me to comprehend why any CIO would enjoy working for a CFO or how these organizations will be able to recruit the right people for these positions. With cybersecurity becoming critical for CIOs, these reporting relationships are long overdue for a change.

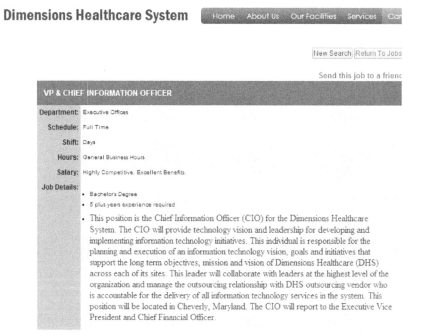

The following ad is also a Director of IT position dressed up as a CIO. The position reports to the CFO creating a natural conflict between the requirements of the role to be strategic but being overruled all the time by the tactical view of the CFO. The CIO salary will also be depressed due to the lower rank and the person will not have proper access to the Provost and other VP level people who will be the CIO's primary clients. Chances are very high the focus will be on the network infrastructure and maintenance – note the highlighting of the wired and wireless networks.

Chief Information Officer

☐ SHARE 🅕🆈✉ _ 💬 📧 Email 🖨 Print

Wingate University is seeking a Chief Information Officer (CIO). A newly created position, the CIO will bring strong strategic leadership and vision for information technology at the University's three campuses and be responsible for all elements of information technology for the student, academic and administrative networks, including wired and wireless infrastructure. The successful candidate will possess strong interpersonal and presentation skills and have a proven track record with several years of experience managing information technology, preferably in a higher education setting. A master's degree or higher in technology or related field is preferred. The position will report to the Vice President of Business, CFO. Interested applicants should submit a letter of interest, resume and contact information of three professional references to hr@wingate.edu. Review of applications will begin immediately. This position will be open until filled. More information about the University can be found at www.wingate.edu. EOE.

Master's degree or higher in technology or related field.

What appears to be happening is that organizations have decided to eliminate the Director of IT title and simply adopt the Chief Information Officer title so they can say they have one. But they have not made all the required changes in authority or compensation or their recruiting methods to ensure that the person they hire is really qualified to serve in these strategic positions. In many organizations, the Director of Networks or other similar level positions have been retitled as a Chief Information Security Officer.

Some organizations have split up the roles of security and privacy and actually have a Chief Information Security Officer and a Chief Privacy Officer (CPO) creating serious confusion and conflict within the organization. They typically hire lawyers in the CPO positions and a technology person in the CISO positions. Instead of combining the salaries and hiring the right person, they have purposefully depressed the salaries of both positions and will have trouble recruiting for both positions.

Associate Vice Chancellor- Chief Information Officer

University of Wisconsin-Milwaukee

SHARE   Email   Print

The University of Wisconsin-Milwaukee (UWM), a doctoral/research intensive University, is Wisconsin's premier public urban university, offering a comprehensive liberal arts and professional education at the undergraduate and graduate level to its 30,000 students. UWM takes pride in being a student-centered institution that is deeply committed to diversity in its student body, faculty, staff, and programs. UWM, a 104-acre campus, is located on Milwaukee's upper east side in one of the city's most attractive residential areas.

Responsibilities: The Associate Vice Chancellor for Information Technology is a member of the Chancellor's administration at UWM, serves on the Chancellor's cabinet, and actively engages in information technology (IT) planning with all administrative and academic units of the university. This position reports directly to the Vice Chancellor for Finance and Administrative Affairs and serves as the university's Chief Information Officer (CIO). The CIO has overall responsibility for the delivery and integration of IT services at UWM and provides leadership and direction to the Division of University Information Technology Services (UITS) and works collaboratively with campus constituent groups in setting priorities for the deployment of IT in support of the teaching, research, learning, service and administrative goals of the university.

The CIO will provide leadership and vision in determining long-term IT needs and provide overall leadership in the planning, development and implementation of leading-edge IT for the university. In addition to establishing and implementing short-and long-range departmental goals, objectives, policies, and operating procedures, the CIO will direct and manage computing and information technology strategic plans, policies, and programs for IT services, network communications, and management information services to accomplish University goals and objectives.

The CIO will develop strategic plans and implement the objective of the IT needs of the

The ad above is quite interesting because it states that the CIO is a member of the Chancellor's cabinet – which means the position should be at the Vice Chancellor level – but it also states that the position is a direct report to the Vice Chancellor of Finance and Administrative Affairs. The problems are the following: 1) the position reports to the administrative side of the institution even though the mission of the institution is academic; 2) the position is one level below all other members on the Chancellor's cabinet ensuring lower empowerment and compensation; and 3) there will be a natural tension between finance driving IT rather than the mission driving IT strategy.

The saddest part of these incongruent reporting relationships is that when a problem happens, the CIO will be in the direct line of fire.

The Importance of Ethics & Integrity During Hiring

During the next few years as organizations scramble to hire a chief information security officer they should carefully screen for ethics and integrity during the interview process. After learning about the candidate selection process in several organizations and after listening to a few anecdotes from several major search organizations, I was puzzled to learn this was not happening. Yet, in my opinion, these are the most important character traits for a CISO to possess.

Here is a story to illustrate the point: An organization wanted to hire a CISO, and it gave its search firm a strict range for the salary. The search firm duly used the range to screen out potential applicants. Several highly qualified candidates honestly admitted the range was too low, and they chose not to interview for the position.

After several rounds of interviews and discussions with the remaining candidates, one emerged as the strongest and received an offer at the highest point on the salary range. The candidate balked, saying that it was lower than his current compensation; he suggested a number 10 percent higher than the offer. Since no other candidate was strong enough, the organization met the candidate's demand. The candidate then turned around and used the offer to obtain a salary increase from his current organization, and he turned down the new organization.

Neither the search firm nor anyone in the organization looking for the CISO was happy about this outcome. What I found most interesting is that, even after the salary range was increased, the search firm did not go back to all the highly qualified candidates who had been previously screened out simply because of the salary range to ask them if they wished to be considered now.

No one appeared to realize that the chosen candidate had been unethical for the following reasons:

1. Though he knew he would not accept something within the advertised range, he had told the search firm he was comfortable with the range and went through the interview process, thus misleading his potential employer.

2. He failed to inform his current employer in good faith that he would like a raise. Instead, he used the new offer to obtain a raise, thus creating a hostage situation with his current employer -- hardly a recipe for maintaining trust in a highly sensitive position.

Events like this happen all the time, and there appears to be a cultural acceptance of negotiating the best offer you can. In general, I agree with the principle of negotiating for the best offer. However, it must be done in an ethical manner. Subtle exchanges during the process reveal a lot about a candidate's character. This candidate may have ruined his future prospects with his current organization, as well. Though the organization opted to keep him since he held them hostage, the organization may make contingency plans for his future departure. In my opinion, it would be negligent not to do so.

Organizations need to ensure that screening for ethics and integrity is a key component of the CISO hiring process. I would not dream of hiring a CISO with weak ethics, and I would have turned down this candidate the moment he asked for something above the strictly advertised range, since he had already agreed to accept an offer within the range. In addition, if the range was increased, I would have asked the recruiting firm to include all the qualified candidates who had previously been screened out simply because of salary range.

To me, ethics and integrity are the most important character traits for a CISO. This is a highly sensitive position, with access and deep knowledge of the security issues of the entire organization; how can someone with questionable ethics be appropriate? If my CISO has weak ethics and integrity, is my organization really going to be secure?

Negotiating CIO & CISO Salaries

Organizations must ensure that CIO and CISO salaries are in line with other executive compensation in the organization. Candidates have to research the organization and ask questions to find out how the offer compares with what other company executives are making.

For the CIO job, where the position reports will define both the true nature of the position and the level of compensation. If, for example, the position reports to the chief financial officer, you will not be a member of the cabinet and your salary is likely to be significantly less than the CFO's pay. This is most likely a director of IT position dressed up with a CIO title. Probably the organization views IT as a cost center rather than as a strategic asset driving revenue. Ask why the CIO reports to the CFO. You may very well find that other C-level executives drive technology decisions and your job is to simply run, support, or integrate these systems -- an operational and not very strategic role.

Some time ago, when I was grappling with this issue, a CFO friend showed me GuideStar.org, a valuable resource he used to judge whether the salary offered was fair and comparable to other C-level executives in the organization. This free website contains the IRS Form 990 filings for the past three years for non-profit organizations. The database includes most universities, religious organizations, healthcare organizations, public and community services, as well as charity organizations.

The IRS 990 filings provide information on the financial stability of the organization as well as compensation for its highest paid people. These data are very valuable in figuring out whether the salary offer for one position is comparable to other executives. Check the filings for all three years to estimate future salary increase potential by looking at the organization's past history of increases.

If a CIO will be a member of the president's cabinet and your offer is significantly lower than other executives, asking about this disparity will often reveal interesting information, which may cause you to have second thoughts about the position. In one case, an organization offered the CIO $50,000 less than the CFO. After questioning, the organization revealed that although the position was a member of the president's cabinet, officially it dual-reported to two other C-level executives -- one of which was the CFO. Not a very comfortable setup!

In the case of a CISO, the offer should be comparable to the CIO's compensation. Organizations -- and candidates for the CISO role -- need to know that the CISO carves out the most complex technical, policy, and operational responsibilities of the CIO in all IT and systems areas. This complex position will require an extremely strong technical, policy, and people management background -- usually more complex than the CIO role. The role also carries with it a high level of career risk compared with all other IT positions within the organization.

The position deals with all parts of the organization. The CISO requires a solid background in all technical areas, including challenging industry certifications. The person will need to be familiar with compliance requirements for applicable security and privacy laws along with a strong background in risk management principles. The CISO also needs strong communications and leadership skills because areas and people influenced will not report to the position. The CISO will manage hundreds of projects and deal with security audits and incidents.

Sometimes an organization will hire a CISO as a true partner for a CIO. It might be defined as a deputy CIO role. At times, the person will be hired to shield others and to serve as the person to be blamed in the event of a major security incident. For a CISO candidate, it will be very important to assess whether this is the case during the interview process. Ask the question: Who is responsible for security in the organization? If the answer is the CISO, that is a warning sign. If the answer is everyone in the organization, you are dealing with an organization that has a better understanding of this role.

Developing a Cybersecurity Program

So how should a CIO or a CISO develop an enterprise cybersecurity program? An organizational cybersecurity program requires three types of controls: technology, policy, and people controls -- which must be managed, monitored and improved over time. This established teaching model in the cybersecurity or information assurance discipline recognizes that technology and policy controls are not sufficient. People within an organization have access to sensitive and protected information; this access can be purposefully or inadvertently exploited to compromise information confidentiality, integrity or availability.

A risk management approach which focuses on the organizational mission and focuses limited resources on high priority security threats and opportunities to develop a balanced program is much better (McAdams, 2004). This approach views cybersecurity as a strategic asset and a business opportunity which gives the organization a competitive edge. Executive management is engaged in developing a program which balances technology, policy, and people controls to ensure the best business return.

People controls entail the leadership and management of people for cybersecurity. Though required, policy controls or training and awareness programs are not sufficient to manage the behavior of people. Policy controls define what is allowed or not allowed – at a broad level. Policy and training and awareness programs must be operationalized into the behavior and work practices of everyone. Furthermore, existence of a policy does not ensure enforcement. Nor does it ensure that people will accept cybersecurity as their responsibility.

Focusing on people controls is attractive and important for three main reasons:
- People controls are cheaper than technical controls (Weber, Alcaro, and Ciotti, 2001).
- People controls govern the behavior of people and become stronger over time (Corriss, 2010).
- People controls target a major source of breaches (Probst, et al., 2010).

Habitual cybersecurity behavior within an organization is called a cybersecurity culture. Cybersecurity culture transfers the responsibility and ownership of cybersecurity from information custodians to every user.

Everyone has a stake in the success of the cybersecurity program and actively participates in improving the environment. In addition, everyone actively promotes and monitors adherence by others and enthusiastically transfers and reinforces these behaviors to new team members (Corriss, 2010). Although such a culture can develop organically over time, executive management is essential in fostering a cybersecurity culture which engages all layers of the organization to drive key values through the organization (Embse, Desai, & Ofori-Brobbey, 2010).

Empowerment and technology education are two factors which help people accept cybersecurity as their responsibility. As people become more proficient in the use of technology, organizations reap the added benefit of increased productivity and innovation – allowing the practice of cybersecurity to be a revenue driver instead of a cost center.

Since low cost and easy access has democratized technology, technical proficiency and habitual practice of cybersecurity has become essential in people's work and personal lives; the demarcation between work and personal lives has become difficult to distinguish. Instead of training people on effective use of technology, many organizations prevent users from performing routine functions on their computers in the name of security. This is similar to giving people a car while disabling important features such as cruise control, windshield wipers or even the ability to fill the gas tank.

Such restrictions drive up support costs and deprive people from using technology effectively; it also limits their ability to learn. Users do not feel trusted and are unable to experiment or innovate as new tools become available. The technology support organization feels overworked and understaffed and does not enjoy servicing repetitive mundane requests.

Sanguine in their belief that technology controls will protect them, users tend to take undue risks and fall victim to social engineering attacks. When a breach occurs, users fault the security organization. A contentious relationship develops between users and the information security organization – and the information security organization is viewed as the "Department of No". The situation fosters a culture where users purposefully bypass organizational security or surreptitiously bring in their own technology in order to exercise better control and get their work done. Sometimes they leave the organization.

On the other hand, users in an empowered organization are more conscious and engaged in information security (Mercuri, 2004). There is a collaborative relationship between users and the information security organization (Hassell & Weidenbeck, 2004). Users recognize and accept cybersecurity as their responsibility and use the resources of the cybersecurity organization to educate themselves on technology. They experiment and innovate and cybersecurity practices become part of their normal behavior. They learn to clean malware, recognize deviations from normal performance and adopt a cybersecurity culture in their work and personal lives.

Examples of successful implementations of a desired organizational culture can be found in organizations such as nuclear power plants, aluminum or steel manufacturing plants and healthcare organizations where safety is a paramount organizational value. Financial organizations offer examples of successfully driving risk management as an organizational culture. Information security is similar in concept to safety and risk management. Time tested people management techniques used to foster safety and risk management cultures can also be used to foster a cybersecurity culture (Hasib, 2013).

However, communications used to discuss ideas must be tailored to suit the audience. For example, a discussion of cybersecurity with buzz words relevant to a security practitioner will not resonate with a group of doctors or nurses; a discussion of patient data safety, instead, should be relevant and appealing to this group. Implementing a strategically balanced cybersecurity program with appropriate levels of technology, policy and people controls will not only foster innovation, enhance productivity, and reduce costs for an organization; it will also result in a much happier work environment.

Building Organizational Teamwork

Values define human and organizational culture. A core set of values can become a team culture that guides the behavior of all members. To become a culture, the team must celebrate people who exemplify the group's values, inculcate new members with these values, and actively resist deviations from these tenets (Deal & Kennedy, 1982; Corriss, 2010). Teamwork at every layer of an organization is essential for organizational success.

However, teamwork does not happen automatically. The values and principles must be practiced and made meaningful to each member of the team. In order to build and maintain effective teams, I instituted the following principles *immediately*. Employees internalized these principles via regular discussions of the principles at team meetings, which allowed them to define in their own words the behaviors that represent these values.

- **Integrity:** Integrity is doing the right thing when no one is looking. Though it takes a lifetime to achieve, integrity can be lost in a moment. Organizations with people of integrity have fewer security problems and higher levels of productivity.
- **Quality:** Quality happens when each person focuses on continuous improvement and takes calculated risks. This requires a cultural willingness to celebrate innovative failures as well as successes. A portion of the team's efforts and budget should be spent on research and innovation.
- **Teamwork:** Teamwork is the magic potion that allows ordinary people to achieve extraordinary things: we may not be strong enough to move a large boulder alone, yet concerted efforts by teams built the great pyramids of Egypt. Properly functioning teams reduce an organization's costs.
- **Customer Service:** Happy customers represent the best form of job security. We approach our jobs as though everyone is our customer and in this manner everyone is our boss. We teach our team members to discover from every customer what they need and when they need it. Everyone wants us to do something right away but this is impossible so we must negotiate, explain, and agree on a mutually acceptable delivery schedule and communicate if there will be deviations.

- **Diversity and Engagement:** Our differing expertise, ideas, and experiences are our strongest assets, and our constructive engagement with each other in sharing and debating ideas lead to better decisions. We must create opportunities for everyone to participate. We must be open to listening to other ideas and constructive criticism of our concepts. The final decisions made through a process of constructive conflict are usually stronger decisions with a better analysis and mitigation of risk.
- **Focus on Non-Monetary Rewards:** The work environment must be fun. People usually do not leave a job; they leave bad managers. As managers, we have a limited supply of monetary rewards but an unlimited supply of good will. A simple thank you for a good job; assignment of an important project; opportunity to attend a conference, training session, or to present at an important event; praise for a commendable action; and making people feel good about how they are helping to achieve the organizational mission -- these are all examples of non-monetary rewards that inspire people and help to retain them.

Additionally, as identified by Tuckman (1965) and widely accepted by scholars who study team development and empirically validated by my own personal experience, all teams go through the following four stages:

- **Forming** – initial introductions and a honeymoon period of discovery.
- **Storming** – a period during which team members learn about each other and their various opinions, strengths and weaknesses. This period is usually accompanied by constructive conflict and arguments. This is normal and should be expected. It is vital for team members to express themselves or they will never get to the next stage. They could be vying for roles as the right people for each role is yet to be determined.
- **Norming** – after the constructive debates, team members adjust to each other and their roles which may be an outcome of the storming period. The rules of team engagement are established during this phase and the team is well on its way to the next stage of development.
- **Performing** – this is the coveted phase that every team which has successfully gone through the previous three phases get to. There is significant interdependence and trust between team members. Everyone knows who is covering for whom. Mentor/mentee

relationships are well established and the team is a consistent winner.

Organizational leaders should make the four stages of teamwork well known to everyone in the organization because when they get to the storming phase, it will be vital to know that some conflict is normal – at some point the team will need to get past that. If they cannot get past that stage, they will never become a team.

Additionally the departure or addition of a single member will require the team to go through all four stages once again. However, the second pass usually takes less time since the number of adjustments required is fewer and there are previously well adjusted members who have experienced the process and are available to help others with the process.

By understanding and explaining teamwork and by insisting on using these values and principles in our teams, we enjoyed a very secure environment with highly productive and innovative employees. Our employees were loyal and supportive of the team and organization, and were very happy coming to work every day. I had an extremely high retention rate and received positive feedback from our clients and team members long after our departures from the organizations.

Designing IT Organizations

Before we can have a meaningful discussion about IT organizations, we need to discuss two critical relationships: the one between customer satisfaction and decentralization and the one between support costs and centralization. Let us delve into both a little more.

Customer Satisfaction and Decentralization

As the image below shows, customer satisfaction increases as decentralization increases -- up to a certain point.

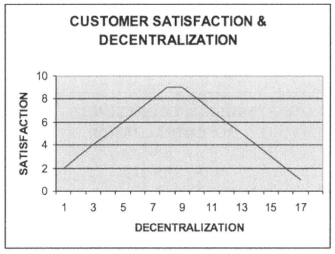

There is a cutoff for customer satisfaction when IT is decentralized.

Many people will argue that the relationship should continue indefinitely -- that if each of us had an IT support person, we would be very happy. This is not true. One key factor is corporate alignment, which represents the degree to which the work meets the institutional mission and adheres to institutional standards. Obviously, if each of us had an IT support person, there would be a complete lack of standards.

Therefore, customer satisfaction increases up to the point of optimal corporate alignment, and then it starts to decline. Finding this optimal point can be a challenge for any organization. Some level of decentralization allows IT to align and embed itself within various business units, while corporate alignment allows some standards to work across the organization -- which is critical for organizational efficiency, collaboration, cohesion and success.

As the alignment with the corporate mission decreases, IT organizations aligned with individual business units are created with independent and redundant layers of management. Standards erode, and it becomes very expensive and difficult to implement corporate applications and provide access to all of the organization's computing resources. Even though customer satisfaction has started to decline at this point, politics (usually of the very ugly kind) take over, and IT organizations begin to criticize one another to win political support and maintain user allegiance. They use customer dissatisfaction as a weapon, and everyone wastes time and energy in mud-slinging contests. I have even seen this phenomenon lead to the demise of organizations.

Support Costs and Decentralization

As this image shows, support costs increase as decentralization increases.

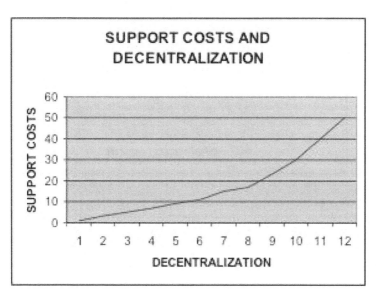

The less centralized the IT structure is, the more it costs organizations.

Implementing corporate applications requires additional customizations and workarounds. Deployments suffer lengthy delays as the company accommodates varying technical approaches. Since each independent organization requires additional layers of management, costs spiral out of control.

Furthermore, since separate environments need to be maintained, they require additional hardware and software, thus escalating an organization's costs and staff requirements. For example, a centralized company may need two servers to support a particular IT service, but supporting the same service in separate organizations could require 12 servers, which means more machines, more software, and more support staff. It is also very difficult for smaller organizations to hire IT personnel with different skill sets. Some organizations can afford an array of skills, but others end up sacrificing and doing without.

This relationship could lead us to believe that organizations should centralize their IT management to control costs. However, too much centralization without recognition of geographic or business unit needs is not good for the organization. Hidden support costs increase when, in the absence of adequate support, employees and business unit leaders perform, support, and manage IT beyond their normal assigned duties. Such costs are difficult to measure, but we must recognize this tendency in designing our IT organization.

Leadership and Teamwork

Good teams require good leaders. Teamwork does not happen in the absence of leadership. We cannot combine a bunch of people and expect them to work together without a clear recognition of elected or appointed leadership. Multiple IT organizations cannot operate as a team unless they report to a single team leader.

Modern Versus Traditional IT Organizations

Traditional computing environments tended to be datacenter-oriented and highly centralized. Modern organizations recognize that the network has become the computing environment for people. By its very nature, the network is distributed, and the computing capacity of an organization is geographically dispersed. While some high risk functions should be centralized, the bulk of IT support should be distributed and closer to the people they serve.

Fair Worker Compensation is Critical

One of the keys for any successful organization is a fair compensation scheme – such that complete transparency in salaries can be possible. Since 2009, I have observed organizations seeking incredibly precise and sophisticated skills for their IT positions, but not paying the appropriate compensation to go along with them.

At first, I chalked it up to the state of the economy: Perhaps, due to the increased supply of highly skilled-workers, wages had dropped. But as the economy improves, I see this trend continuing. Organizations often want IT workers with high-level certifications such as CISSP, ITIL, Six Sigma, PMP, and others -- but these organizations also want to pay salaries that are well below market value.

When asked to explain, the usual response is: "This is what we can afford." Asked if they are having trouble filling the positions, the response is: "Yes, we have interviewed several people within the range and found them to be unqualified. We have been unable to fill the position for several months." And then we see articles discussing the so-called "skills gap."

Multiply this scenario across hundreds of organizations, and what we have is actually an artificial skills gap. Granted in some cases organizations may have a true skills gap, and may need to invest in training workers to solve this problem. But at salaries of $10 to $18 an hour, it appears unlikely that a skilled IT employee will have a decent living wage in most major cities in the United States.

On the other hand, the spiraling cost of education -- despite technological advances to fix this -- is putting higher education out of reach for many families. Some organizations recognize their compensation is under-market, but cannot adjust due to budget issues. So, they hire someone they will need to educate. Unfortunately, organizations frequently lack the people needed to train this person, and think that the new hire will learn on the job.

Who will train a chief information officer (CIO) or a chief information security officer (CISO)? How is someone supposed to learn this role on the job, particularly in a highly-complex organization?

Sometimes, organizations hire someone unqualified without realizing it. About a year later, they decide they are not getting the right value from the role. So, they make organizational changes; sometimes they alter the reporting relationships, and sometimes they even get rid of the role.

Despite the difficulty in hiring, organizations appear to be reluctant to train people. Failure to hire the right candidate simply because of money is a major mistake. Hiring the wrong candidate will cost the organization much more, and may cause good workers to leave. Quality employees want fair market compensation, and in return, they will give value back to the organization. This is simple management.

Artificial budget reasons are leading to an artificial skills gap -- the modern equivalent of "penny wise, pound foolish." This needs to stop. I believe it's hurting the organizations, it's hurting the work force, and it's hurting the economy. Long-term, it may even create challenges in global competition.

Organizational leaders must eliminate the artificial skills gap. It's the ethical and patriotic thing to do. If you cannot find quality employees at a particular salary range, you *must* adjust your range. Analyze every position's salary and ensure compensation is fair and market-based. Without such a basis, the problem will continue to exacerbate.

If you do manage to hire someone below market, you will be unable to retain the person for long. When a good employee leaves an organization, there is significant cost -– knowledge loss, training costs, interviewing and recruiting costs, as well as productivity loss for all the positions that the person was connected to within the organization. Underpaying workers does not equate to a skills gap.

Recruiting the Best Team Members

Recruiting IT and cybersecurity staff is not easy. Technology changes so rapidly that if you focus on the wrong things during your recruiting process, you will end up hiring the wrong person. Frequently it will be expensive to recover from a recruiting error.

In addition to writing very specific and detailed job descriptions for IT and cybersecurity staff, I have also seen ads where two dramatically different skill sets are combined into one position making it impossible to find a single person who qualifies. Then they wait months waiting to hire.

My recommended recruiting strategy is completely different. The right IT/cybersecurity candidate for me will have a good foundation but a strong desire for continuous learning and unquestionable ethics and integrity. While I can teach an ethical person technology, unethical people never make a good IT or cybersecurity professional.

Furthermore, technology changes so rapidly that if a person does not have the passion to learn continuously, the person will be obsolete and useless to me very quickly. So focusing on very specific skills is frequently unnecessary because if the foundation is there, you can build upon it.

So how do you screen for ethics and integrity? Your interview set should contain a good number of relevant non-technical questions that allow you to assess this. The following is an example of one of the best hiring decisions I ever made:

In one of my past roles as a CIO, we had an open position for a part-time user support assistant and we wanted to fill it with a student intern from one of the local colleges. Our goal with these positions was to give budding information technology professionals an opportunity to become exposed to the business world and to find their passion within the field.

One candidate stood out for sincerity in her responses. It was clear she was not exaggerating her qualifications beyond what were true, nor was she saying anything just to please us -- her responses were thoughtful, honest and to the point – there was no fluff in any of her responses.

Nearing the end of the interview I asked her, "So where else have you applied for internships?"

She mentioned two other organizations. So I asked, "In what area of IT are those internships?"

"One is in the networking area, and the other is in the database area," she replied.

"Among the three internships, what is your order of preference?" I pursued.

Without flinching at all, she stated, "My first choice is [Company A], my second choice is [Company B]..." Her responses put us in last place.

Without flinching myself, I asked her to explain the reasoning behind her ranking. Methodically, she explained, "[Company A] has the networking internship. I have heard network engineers make a lot of money. I have also heard that database people have strong career prospects."

After her departure, the committee sat down to make a decision. We each had our favorite candidate. Mine was this candidate -- though I was a little surprised to be the only one championing her.

"But she is not even interested in this position -- we are her third choice!" someone protested.

"I am not sure she will enjoy working in user support if she truly wants to be a network engineer or a database analyst," another person added.

"Yes, I agree with these concerns," I said. "But look -- her integrity is beyond question. She was the most honest of all the candidates we saw. Integrity of this level is rare. Yet, it is the most important asset in the IT field. We deal with too much sensitive information. We will be able to trust exactly what she tells us. She will not cover up her mistakes -- she will own up to them and we will be able to correct them.

"Look at how fearlessly she told us the truth about her choices. She was not willing to lie to make us feel good. She also gave us honest answers for her reasons. Thus, if she ends up working here, to be fair to her, we know that we have to expose her to network engineering as well as databases.

"Remember -- she is a young student and she still has to find herself. As part of her internship, we have to teach her that loving her work is more important than pursuing money. She can only be good in something she truly loves. Money will automatically follow quality as she progresses in her career. If we offer her the position, we will tell her we will expose her to our network engineers and database analysts so she can learn about those areas as well. We can give her all three internships right here and we can become her first choice. Once she has exposure to all the areas, she will be in a better position to judge what she truly loves.

"Personally, I would love the opportunity to work with a person of such high integrity at this stage in her career so I can mentor her the right way from the very beginning. She will be a star IT person someday."

Luckily, everyone agreed to give this candidate a chance and she readily accepted. We duly exposed her to network engineering as well as databases and she was able to find herself. She found out that she did not like network engineering. She ended up becoming an excellent business analyst with a strong database background. Her user support role taught her to deal with a wide variety of people and understand what they did. It also allowed her to polish her leadership skills, which became very important in her career.

After graduation, she ended up going to a different organization because we did not have the right position for her. A few years later she competed for a different position in a different organization I was running. Once again her integrity came through during the interview and everyone agreed to bring her on board. She had never worked on the exact systems we were running – but she had the foundation to build on. She quickly learned everything she needed to learn, found and fixed the flaws in the system and quickly validated everyone's faith in her integrity and discipline. To build a strong team, this is the type of team members we need to hire.

Retaining Great Employees

We cannot build great teams without retaining great people. We all agree that it is not easy to find great people. Some turnover is healthy and normal for any organization, and we need to plan for that. However, losing great people hurts the organization significantly. It can even mean the difference between success and failure. So why is it that managers and leaders do not work hard enough to retain great people after they have worked so hard to find them? Retaining great people is far easier and cheaper than to recruit.

I have frequently heard the excuse, "We simply cannot afford to keep paying them higher compensation." Having worked most of my career in non-profit organizations, I know the challenges of market competition and the limits of monetary compensation. I also know that there will be occasions when your team members will simply outgrow your organization and must find something else to attain the next level in their careers. As leaders, we should never hold someone back.

The professional success of every person on our team is our moral and professional responsibility. If someone's professional growth can only be achieved outside our organization, we should be willing to facilitate that. There should be open dialogue between us and our team members.

If they are planning a transition outside the organization, they must let us know without fear of retribution. That is the only way we can plan for a smooth succession so it does not hurt the organization. I am not a big fan of two week notices. All my team members have always felt comfortable discussing their professional growth ideas and plans with me and I have actively mentored and worked with them to help them achieve their career goals. In most cases, this growth was possible within the organization.

The only time I would not even try to retain someone is when that person brings me a competitive offer and then asks for a raise or a promotion. That is hostage taking. This person cannot be trusted and must be transitioned out as quickly as possible. Retaining the person will negatively affect the rest of the team. Integrity and trust is critical in any IT organization – it has become even more important in this new world of cybersecurity. Job hoppers are not very desirable team members.

Compensation must be fair and market based – in line with the industry or the type of organization. Artificially depressed compensation levels with lame budget excuses such as "This is all we can afford" simply will not work for long. During depressed market conditions we may find some good people – but we will not retain them when the market balances out -- as it always does.

So what are some of the ways to retain good people? Here is what I did – I focused on making sure they are happy. Great employees are most motivated through non-monetary rewards. Although we have a limited supply of monetary rewards, we have an unlimited supply of non-monetary rewards.

Great employees are usually working in a field because it is their passion. It is their calling and they love doing what they do – and that is why we hired them. Remember? So if we spend more time making sure our employees are happy, we will get amazing amounts of productivity out of them. We will have their unwavering loyalty and they will frequently turn down higher financial rewards in order to remain in the organization where they can be happy and creative, and can rest assured that they will always be treated fairly. Matter of fact, if they are happy, they will not look around.

Great employees want to be happy when they come to work. IT people are very creative people and we must liberate them and allow their creative juices to flow. Their greatest satisfaction comes from knowing they have made a contribution to the organization. They need to know how their work ties back to the mission of the organization. This makes the work far more meaningful for them.

Chances are very high, your organization's mission attracted them to your organization. Even if this was not the case initially, once they are motivated by your mission they will be on auto-pilot. It is our job to enable this translation -- continuously. They should know how their work is furthering the mission of the organization. This will also help them to bond with the organization. The stronger their bond with the organization, the better chances you will have of retaining them.

We must be generous with non-monetary rewards. We must look for opportunities to give them away with sincerity and gratitude. A new project, opportunity to implement an original idea, a public recognition of a new idea, a celebratory luncheon, an opportunity to present at a conference or in front of organizational executives -- are all examples of non-monetary rewards that motivate people. Being stingy with "thank you" notes, commendation letters, or congratulatory handshakes does us no good. Generosity with these non-monetary rewards will unleash creativity and help retain great people.

Performance evaluations must be accurate, fair, and mutually agreed upon, and outstanding performance must be rewarded with better pay increases. We should never wait until the evaluation paperwork needs to be completed for employees to know where they stand. You should already have planned projects and targets. If they have been completing them, they should already know where they stand. If something needs to be adjusted because of some emergency, make those adjustments in the work plan immediately. All performance targets should be realistic and completely within the employee's control. No one should ever be penalized for circumstances beyond their control.

Our employees must be able to trust that we will protect them – if they have done nothing wrong – they should not be arbitrarily terminated. The fear of an arbitrary layoff can be deadly for any organization. Yet I see so many organizations use this tool to manage their finances from year to year. Termination for cause is a different story. However, I have never laid anyone off in my career. Nor did I ever allow a higher level manager to lay off someone in my organization due to some arbitrary company-wide 10% layoff.

If CEOs and CFOs are having trouble making numbers meet, why are they never laying themselves off first? Wouldn't it save the organization more money? Isn't it their incompetence and failure to manage risks that got the organization in the financial mess in the first place? Yes I have heard the excuse of market conditions. I would argue that these executives are paid to plan for these contingencies. If they cannot plan, they should not be in their jobs. Making the entire organization suffer for their incompetence is wrong.

The 10% across the board cut is an executive's failure to make tough decisions. As we saw in the case of the competitors of Southwest Airlines, it will be deadly for the organization in the long run. People who are doing their jobs should not be laid off. In every company, there are some people who are not doing their jobs. Employees who do not have a work ethic should be dismissed. We have to be loyal to the employees who are loyal to the organization.

There was a time during my career when I was reporting to a CFO and I was told we were having a 10% across the board layoff. I was told to lay off one person in my organization – I was even told which person I had to lay off. After a couple of days of careful thought, I gave the CFO my decision. Since the layoff was purely a financial matter and my salary was higher than my team member's salary, I volunteered to be laid off so that the organization could save more money.

Taken aback, the CFO told me that was not an option. I then pointed out that if we looked carefully around the entire organization, there were several people in various departments who were not doing any work at all – and were actually causing problems. I also gave him the financial and productivity analysis of my proposed cuts in other departments (in writing) and showed him how that would make better financial and strategic sense for the organization.

My organization was already lean. Over the years, we had taken on so much responsibility without adding any staff members that laying off any member would lead to a complete failure for my entire team. For coverage and risk management reasons, each member of my team had become deeply intertwined with all other members of the team and the permanent removal of anyone would result is a major breakdown for the team. It would be like playing baseball without a position player. Since I was doomed to fail anyway, better to resign early than to fail later.

Another key is professional development. While some professional development activities may cost money there are many conferences and training that are available for free. Most conferences will allow complimentary attendance for presenters. Encourage your employees to present at these conferences.

As IT managers and leaders, it is our job to foster the professional growth of everyone who works on our team. If we do not do this, we are failing as leaders. If their skills atrophy or their certifications expire because we are not allowing them any opportunity to earn their continuing education credits, how can it be helpful to the organization? It is professional malpractice!

I have had many discussions on the topic of training with both employees and managers. Many IT managers fear certifications will make their employees more marketable and allow them to find better opportunities.

Employees are frustrated that their managers do not allow them to grow; so they leave to learn and grow professionally.

When I was negotiating my first budget as a CIO, I asked for and received $2,000 per year for every employee on my team. It was part of the compensation structure that could only be used for conferences or training. It required consultation with supervisors and could be used for certification fees or for continuing education credits. Since some training were more expensive, employees were allowed to trade among themselves. They could give up training dollars for one year in order to gain them back from the recipient in the following year. On several occasions, I was able to recruit someone simply because I had this guaranteed annual training benefit.

This arrangement was an amazing motivator for the team. It kept the skills of my staff growing and they were able to sharpen their thinking, discuss issues with peers in other institutions, and apply the knowledge toward innovation within our organization. In nearly 10 years, no one left the organization -- they were so happy with the environment, their professional growth, and the mutual support they received from each other that the thought of looking around never entered their minds.

I could never have foreseen future events, but in late 2009 and early 2010, when an organization where I served as a CIO was abolished during very tough economic conditions, every member of my team found a new job as a result of their up-to-date skills, certifications, discipline, and leadership skills.

Finally – we must recognize the power of the social network in the workplace. As humans we are all social beings. People usually develop strong bonds at work and it is our job to foster and encourage that. This social network creates a sense of belonging. It makes collaboration easier. Our employees are happier and more productive. The more friends people have at work, the more attached they feel to the organization and the harder it becomes for good people to leave.

Engaging Our Team in Innovation

Innovation is critical for every organization's success. Yet, many organizations fail to innovate -- and this failure is an expensive oversight -- something that causes billions of dollars in lost worker productivity in the United States. But innovation does not have to be dramatic or earth shattering. In fact, according to the Japanese Kaizen concept, most innovation occurs through iteration, and small, incremental adjustments.

Empowerment, teamwork, collaboration, and communication (including constructive criticism) are critical elements for allowing such incremental adjustments to occur within teams and organizations. During my twelve year tenure as CIO at two different organizations, I used a simple technique to produce remarkable results. I instituted regular team meetings with rotating meeting chairs and note takers for each meeting. Everyone took turns at leading meetings, taking notes, writing and distributing the minutes, and setting the agenda. This system ensured the following:

1. Everyone had the opportunity to practice leadership, meeting management, facilitating discussions, and managing time.
2. Silence during these meetings was not an option -- everyone had to express an opinion around every issue. Constructive debates surrounded ideas, not the person proposing an idea. The goal was to ensure a bad idea could be polished into a good one. To move forward, the team had to support and own any idea.
3. Each person could practice the art of listening and capturing the proceedings of a meeting in order to take notes and produce the minutes.
4. Every employee had to know the important issues and the priorities in order to produce a reasonable agenda for a meeting.
5. People improved their own skills by observing others.
6. Team meetings did not depend on the presence of any anointed team leader and the absence of a single person did not affect the team.
7. Everyone knew what everyone else was working on, the problems and issues we faced, and could offer suggestions and solutions: Success for everyone became a team sport.
8. Each team member was required to lead some effort and utilize other members of the team as resources for the project. Thus, they

    learned project leadership as well as project membership, and the discipline of dividing their attention between multiple projects.

9.   Members had the opportunity to prepare and make both formal and informal presentations -- each had an opportunity to learn and practice the art of making presentations within a protected and trustworthy environment -- with no personal risk.

My primary focus was to ensure people had fun at these meetings and that the team adopted and internalized a few key principles such as leadership, integrity, teamwork, continuous learning, and customer service. To confirm the team understood what each of these principles meant, we devoted a short discussion on a team principle at the end of each meeting. The team developed a list of key behaviors giving meaning to each principle, and adopted the list of behaviors as team ideals.

Of course, the amazing by-product of this system was a high degree of innovation -- and an amazing level of productivity -- all due to the high level of leadership, engagement, and teamwork everyone exhibited. Since the entire team vetted everyone's ideas, the probability of success improved dramatically. With multiple brains involved, it did not take long to percolate the innovative ideas that would lead to success. Small adjustments and iterations made after collective thought made several complex projects possible in record time -- some were projects that originally had been thought too complex to be done internally. Even student interns and new employees became rapidly engaged into the work environment due to this simple technique.

After the first meeting, I never led the sessions. Instead, I coached and encouraged others. Because of this, the team clearly recognized that leadership was not inherent in a position; rather, anyone can be a leader. Since anyone, including me, could be used as a resource in anyone's project, people learned it was most important to have the right resources for their projects. They learned to negotiate and coax getting commitment of those resources from each empowered employee – who was free to allocate time to projects they would enjoy. Even better, we all had a fun time.

Accepting Innovative Failures

Innovative failures and mistakes are bound to happen to the person who takes the highest number of risks and tries the highest number of innovations. People who do nothing make no mistakes. People who do the most work are likely to make a few errors. Innovation inherently carries with it a risk of failure. It is best to recognize likely failures early. It is dangerous to egotistically continue spending money and effort on implementing a bad idea for fear of organizational retribution.

Is it appropriate to fire someone for a mistake? Should we penalize someone for failure in an innovative venture? I would argue against it. Such an atmosphere can be deadly for innovation for any organization. It can actually ruin an IT organization. Organizations and IT leaders that do not tolerate mistakes -- or innovative failures -- will stagnate. Fear of retribution will reduce productivity and creativity and will cause the most valuable and innovative employees to leave.

We should never penalize people for mistakes. Instead we should teach people to manage the risks of innovation and ensure that they take adequate precautions to recover from a mistake or an innovative failure. A good example is making a backup of the system before making a change and ensuring a way to reinstate the system to its original state. Another example is discussing a high-risk action or plan with other qualified people before execution. Even highly skilled doctors ask for second and third opinions. This is simple due diligence.

Risk management has to be part of the standard operating procedure. If a person fails to follow this procedure, we may have an argument for consequences. It is important to ensure that people feel comfortable owning up to errors so that appropriate corrective action can be applied and people can learn how to avoid the mistake in the future.

Quality control reduces errors and mistakes. All members of a team should work toward an atmosphere where people help each other avoid errors and share lessons learned. We should never hide or gloss over bad events.

A couple of years ago I had the pleasure of listening to Dr. Jamshed Irani, former CEO of Tata Steel, who turned the company around in the late 80s and early 90s by engaging the entire organization in a culture of innovation. One of the ideas that emerged during his tenure was Tata's practice of giving "Dare to Try" awards for innovative ideas that were operationally unsuccessful. Failed ideas teach us what does not work and provide us the opportunity to think critically so that the next idea has a better chance of success.

Since there is an inherent risk of failure in trying anything new, we should ensure that all team members are free to speak their minds and constructively criticize any new idea -- even if the idea comes from the team leader. People closest to the leader are more likely to see the flaws in the idea -- they may even be more qualified to evaluate the risks of the idea appropriately.

After various perspectives have been provided and everyone has had an opportunity to punch holes in the idea, chances are very high that the final decision will be stronger, with more risks identified and appropriately addressed. People should not feel bad about saying something incorrect. Only people who say nothing are always correct. People who actively participate in discussions are bound to say something incorrect once in a while. It is important to recognize and acknowledge that this is normal.

So let us set our people free to innovate, create, and debate; and let our organizations enjoy the wonderful rewards of such an atmosphere.

The Critical Role of User Support

Many organizations tend to ignore user support. They frequently outsource it and sometimes they staff it with people who are not capable of truly helping users or training them at every opportunity. People forget that one of the key roles of user support is to teach people how to help themselves.

I began my career in user support, where I discovered my true love and vocation: the information technology field. Investments in technology unleashes high returns only when users are able to use the technology effectively. Thus, effective user support and training is essential for organizations. Almost everyone in the IT organization should be engaged in supporting users at some level.

Supporting end users is one of the best ways to meet our colleagues and learn about what they do in the organization. It allows us to sharpen our problem-solving skills. Most importantly, it teaches us to deal with people with all kinds of personalities. Some will have egos and attitudes; some may even have rude tempers. It was the best way for me to meet some of the nicest people in the organization and discover the organization's best leaders. The key to success as a CIO is to make friends with the organization's best leaders – and the best people. They become our champions for success.

Working in user support tends to be highly stressful, and people can experience rapid burnout. That is why it is best to rotate out of a full-time user support role into a mixed project/user support role as our career progresses. It is also why most user support organizations need to be tiered. At the first level, we may have a call center, which initiates a trouble ticket and solves routine problems and issues. This is usually treated as an entry-level position and can be staffed with newcomers.

For most IT organizations, user support jobs are low-risk positions that can be used to vet and groom workers. This level is perfect for interns who are smart and curious and crave opportunities to experience the business world. Students from any major university can be successful in this role if they enjoy meeting people and solving puzzles. After all, user support is an endless supply of puzzles to solve.

Since the primary focus of user support is customer service, we learn that customer negotiations are an integral part of delivering great service. Customer service is a matter of managing expectations. Every user support professional has limited time and several problems to solve simultaneously. Everyone wants their problems solved first. But, this is impossible, so we must assess the problem's impact and negotiate a timeframe which the client can accept *and* a schedule we can meet. Ultimately, this is one of the key factors in determining how satisfied the client will be. Client perception is paramount.

Listening is another important skill. How accurately and precisely we collect information about the problem will be critical in solving the problem quickly. The solution we provide must address the problem without creating a new one. We must learn to stay calm and positive. Our attitude is likely to influence the person we are interacting with and will help us collect better information. Staying calm will often calm down an agitated client.

We must practice the art of follow-up -- asking the client if the solution solved the problem – and did the problem stay solved or come back. Was there a new problem? This is our opportunity to establish credibility and rapport with the customer. These are important assets that we will be able to bank for future negotiating advantage. If people have been happy with our solutions and follow through in the past, they are more likely to give us a generous timetable with the next problem, because they have more faith in our ability to deliver. It takes time to build a positive reputation.

We will also learn how to leverage the various resources at our disposal effectively -- such as other team members, knowledge bases, and Internet resources such as vendor sites and support forums. No matter how far we rise, the lessons we learned in user support will follow us throughout our career. Granted, we may have different types of problems to solve, but if we are in the field of IT, we will always have to support our clients properly. Ignoring this area is a major mistake.

Helping Employees Succeed

To run effective organizations we must help everyone in our organization succeed. How exactly can this be achieved? The other day, I was talking to a few undergraduate students who were stressing over applying for the right internships, which could lead to a job – perhaps in the same company. They were asking for tips on achieving success in the IT field.

Reflecting on my own experience, I asked, "What if the exact area where you will achieve success has not been invented yet? And what if colleges aren't teaching what you will need to know for success in that area?" "This is what happened to me," I continued, "It took me more than 30 years to earn my doctoral degree because I had to wait for the field to be invented," I joked.

Every worker in any company must be focused on several key things that will help them mature, grow and succeed. Organizational leaders should concentrate on ensuring that all workers in the organization can achieve the following goals. They also need to recruit people who can achieve the following.

Be happy – we have to be happy and excited about what we do. Over time, our preferences may change and we need to be prepared to adjust. However, without happiness, we cannot excel at anything and without excellence we cannot attain the monetary rewards we seek. Money automatically follows excellence.

Be the best – quality and current skills in our field matter not only for financial rewards but also for job security. While we cannot control what managers and others around us do, we fully control our own actions and can focus on achieving excellence in anything we do.

Be ambitious – people and circumstances will frequently attempt to encircle us with limitations. We do not have to accept them. No one knows our limitations better than us. We should never let others define our limitations. So we should dare to dream and fiercely attempt to overcome these limitations in pursuit of our dreams.

Be strategic – every organization has a mission and when we work for any organization, we have to understand and promote that mission. We need to know how our work fits into the mission and we should be able to explain this to others in simple language. Without this translation our work may never be meaningful to us or appreciated by others.

Be aware – since everything is continuously changing around us, we need to assimilate and adapt to these changes. These changes may present new opportunity or require that we learn something new.

Be curious – since the IT field is a field with rapid change, we must learn and update our skills continuously. We must attend conferences, read journals, engage with others, and obtain relevant certifications or advanced degrees.

Be friendly – given the multi-disciplinary nature of most problems, success is usually a team effort. So building relations and being able to work with others in a collaborative and supportive way is critical not only for the success of the organization but also for our own success.

Finally, be thankful – we must always recognize that countless people made our success possible. Parents, grandparents, teachers, relatives, friends, co-workers, generous donors – they all paved the way for us. We should always treasure these people -- and be thankful. Repaying our debts to the specific people who helped us may not be possible – but we can give back -- by helping someone else to succeed. This is the magic of a successful society.

Note: This article was adapted from *"Success in the IT Field: B's Are Also Important."* by M. Hasib, March 2013. (Link: http://www.youtube.com/watch?v=1_dEX0MkHOQ).

A Few Things to Avoid

In this new world where IT needs to align with business goals and be responsive to user needs, the perception we create in the minds of the people in the organizations we serve is critical to our success. Sometimes we may suffer from an "ivory tower" mentality – and feel that users cannot be trained in technology. So we resort to doing everything for them instead of teaching them how to do it. Other times, corporate culture has unwittingly relegated IT far from the core business and has viewed it as a remote keeper of vital but secret (and expensive) knowledge.

I think it is very important to make sure that our organization does not suffer from the following seven deadly sins:

1. **IT is the department of "NO."** IT departments that are not customer oriented usually earn this reputation. The mission of the IT department should be the same as the mission of the organization. We need to find more ways of saying "YES." We need to listen to clients and provide value by enabling them to perform their jobs better through proper use of technology.
2. **IT support is a commodity and not part of the core business and can be easily outsourced.** IT is integral to the core business of most organizations today since we can hardly do anything without IT. Proper support of business applications usually requires deep understanding of the business, and this understanding is not easily outsourced. While outsourcing some aspects of IT should always be considered as an option, it rarely pays to outsource intellectual capital.
3. **Cybersecurity is strictly IT's job.** Within any organization, cybersecurity is everyone's job since everyone has access to protected information and most breaches are a result of human action. Cybersecurity is rooted in risk management and safety. This is a vast, highly interdisciplinary field with three main areas of focus: technology, policy, and people management. Organizations frequently make the mistake of implementing only a few of the technical controls while ignoring the rest. Professionals from a wide variety of backgrounds are needed to work on various aspects of cybersecurity. Psychologists, sociologists, criminologists, computer scientists and engineers, network engineers, business administrators, risk managers, political scientists, lawyers, human

resources personnel, recruiters, lawyers, and people from many other disciplines are involved in an organization's comprehensive cybersecurity program.

4. **Requiring users to change passwords frequently improves security.** This is a favorite for many people working in the IT department of NO. They will make users change passwords frequently, but system administrator passwords will go unchanged for months -- even after systems administration personnel depart the company! Frequent password changes are a major burden on users -- especially if they are forced to use highly complex passwords. People usually solve the problem by writing down their passwords in a conspicuous place, resulting in reduced security. It also drives up the number of support calls and the number of locked out accounts. I am amazed to see IT departments keep user accounts locked out for weeks forcing people to use each other's accounts – just to get their work done. How is this improving security? Passwords are usually compromised through phishing or spyware. Training people to manage and protect passwords and to practice safe computing is a far better idea than forcing them to change passwords frequently. I have observed incredible amounts of productivity lost through locked-out accounts and legitimate users unable to access the system while the Department of NO takes days, weeks and even months to reset passwords and unlock accounts. Any policy that keeps a legitimate user out of the system for longer than 15 minutes is a bad policy and must be changed!

5. **We need IT support to move PCs and to connect projectors.** I have never understood this phenomenon. Using expensive IT people to perform routine tasks such as equipment moves and setup is a total waste of money. Technology has become ubiquitous, and most users are capable of self-help of this type, allowing IT to concentrate on more complex support tasks. Unless there is a requirement to implement specific port-level security, most users can be effectively trained to disconnect and connect computer equipment.

6. **You need an information technology or computer science background to work in IT.** Nothing could be further from the truth. Today every organization is an IT organization – whether we realize this or not. Almost every worker is an IT worker because of the higher level of technical skills required in any job. Most IT professionals do not program any more. Instead they are highly proficient users of technology. Therefore, anyone with a passion can be a technology worker. When I became a network engineer, network engineering was not taught in any of the colleges. Many of

my best employees came from non-IT backgrounds and became successful because of their friendly personalities, discipline, and passion for helping people and learning. Technology changes so rapidly that people can become highly proficient in new technology in a short time. Indeed, they must continue learning or they will become obsolete rather quickly.

7. **The leader of an IT department needs to be technical.** IT department leaders need to understand the business and cultivate strong relations throughout the organization. They need to be able to develop long-term strategies that align with business goals. They need to be able to inspire the IT team to be innovative and helpful. They need to be able to stay current with the industry by networking with other IT leaders. While strong technical skills are not an absolute requirement for IT leaders if we are able to surround ourselves with strong technical people, a complete lack of technical experience will be a major drawback because non-technical executives will not make the best strategic technical choices or understand how to recruit, mentor, and retain good IT people. We must understand the technical people we lead and the organization we serve and function as the primary translator.

Cybersecurity Dangers of Outsourcing

Organizations must recognize the cybersecurity dangers of outsourcing and offshoring. Therefore, I was very happy to see some new words creeping into the business vernacular recently. Words such as insourcing, inshoring, and reshoring are becoming more common. In simple terms, insourcing is the process of bringing contractual and outsourced services back into the organization. Inshoring, or reshoring, brings back contractual and outsourced services or manufacturing from overseas to the US.

There are some positive implications inshoring and reshoring have for information technology and cybersecurity. After all, cybersecurity is complex and challenging enough within the US borders. When multiple nations are involved, this complexity and challenge increase significantly. Here are a few advantages:

Better control over supply-chain management. Integrity and a reliable chain of custody for all components of a system are important aspects of determining its information assurance level or cybersecurity strength. This integrity is especially vital for control systems used in many national critical infrastructures.

International supply-chain management is inherently very complex. On top of that, the need to maintain integrity control of all components in a multinational environment further compounds this complexity -- frequently eliminating, and sometimes exceeding, the original cost advantages of outsourcing.

Better security of intellectual property. Though intellectual property is substantially at risk in any outsourced venture, international outsourcing increases the risk of US intellectual property loss dramatically. There could be loyalty issues, disclosure issues, or data retention issues. Communication links could be subject to unwanted or unknown surveillance. Additionally contractual and legal protections could be difficult to enforce.

Fewer risks to quality. In many cases, we have experienced quality reductions to unacceptable levels in various products and services that have been outsourced to international ventures. This has resulted in a return of these services and products back to the US shores.

Higher availability of the supply chain. International supply chains are frequently affected by international political, economic, and other forces that can negate the expected savings and reduce availability.

Reduced insider threat. Insiders are workers in an organization who have authorized access to systems and information. Inadvertent as well as malicious insider threats to information security are inherently most difficult to deal with. When this threat is spread across multiple countries, the risk is multiplied significantly. Value systems, cultural norms, workforce requirements, and normal everyday life can provide hostile outsiders the ability to foster insider threats. In addition, many types of people controls and legal protections become unreliable or unavailable on foreign soil.

Easier access to US research institutions. Partnerships between government, industry, and US research institutions of higher learning have often been a major driving force behind innovation in technology. Without US-based manufacturing, such partnerships are weakened. Insourcing, inshoring, or reshoring from foreign countries back to the US should provide industry with increased access to US institutions of higher learning.

Fewer international technology transfer issues. Whenever technology leaves US borders, technology export laws are applicable. In addition, the laws of the foreign countries involved have to be considered. These considerations not only increase complexity and costs but can also introduce unacceptable levels of risk.

Reduced international data storage issues. Security of data at rest is always a challenge. When data crosses international borders, additional security considerations usually come into play.

Reduced exposure to international privacy laws. Data residing on foreign soil is subject to the privacy laws of the host country. In addition, US privacy laws may continue to be applicable. Reconciling all applicable laws is a significant challenge.

Empowering Users for Better Security

Diving deeper into the issue of user empowerment and engagement, let me ask: Are users in your organization fully empowered to utilize their computers -- install and update software, define printers, and perform other routine tasks? Or do they have to call the help desk for every little thing they need done, frequently waiting for several days only to be told, "No, we cannot do it" or "It will compromise security" or "It's just not allowed in our organization?"

Having worked in both types of organizations, and having managed the IT environment in an empowered organization as CIO/CISO, I have observed that users in overly restrictive environments have an antagonistic relationship with IT and cybersecurity. They feel cybersecurity is someone else's responsibility. Experimentation and innovation levels are low. IT is usually overworked and understaffed and does not enjoy servicing the majority of requests, since they are mundane and present no new challenges. The typical call volume for service is also very high.

In the empowered organization, users are more conscious of and more engaged in cybersecurity. There is a collaborative relationship with IT, which is viewed as helpful. Users also recognize and accept cybersecurity as their responsibility.

Organizational cybersecurity rests on three pillars: technology, policy, and people. Getting the people part right is very important for any organization. Getting it wrong could hurt the organization in many ways. Users could intentionally bypass security measures they do not view as helpful. They could fail to disclose problems or share concerns. They could suppress important ideas and suggestions that could improve the cybersecurity of the organization.

During a keynote address at the 2012 CISO Executive Summit in Washington, DC, Ira Winkler, CEO of Internet Security Advisors Group, told CISOs to create a collaborative relationship with users to keep IT from being labeled as the "Department of NO." Justin Somaini, CISO of Yahoo, at that time, shared similar experiences during an afternoon keynote. He argued that it was important to get users within the organization to accept information security as their personal responsibility. One key way to accomplish this, he said, is to empower users.

Somaini found very little difference in security between empowered and non-empowered environments. But in my own experience, I have observed more virus infections and security issues in organizations with severe restrictions on user capabilities, primarily because the absence of a security culture promoted unsafe user behavior.

The remarks by Winkler and Somaini made me think of the safety culture I observed at a nuclear power plant early in my career. The organization was run according to key values such as safety, employee empowerment (with a questioning attitude), teamwork, customer service, excellence, and diversity. These values were consciously driven throughout the organization. All employees were empowered to question any order they believed would reduce safety. Supervisors could not penalize employees for such questioning. Everyone was encouraged to think continuously of ways to improve safety. Thus, germination of grassroots ideas from people closest to the work was part of the culture. This produced a highly safety-conscious workforce, superior team spirit, a collaborative relationship between workers and management -- and an excellent safety record.

The same principles could achieve a culture of cybersecurity within an organization. After all, information security isn't much different from safety.

Granted, in a few highly controlled, top-security environments, a high level of empowerment may not be appropriate. Users who work in these environments easily recognize and appreciate the restrictions. However, most enterprises would benefit greatly if a culture of cybersecurity was cultivated throughout the organization. User empowerment and the cultivation of a collaborative relationship between IT and the user community is the key way to foster such a culture.

Implementing Bring Your Own Device

As work and personal lives of workers blend, it becomes increasingly difficult for workers to carry around multiple devices for their work and personal lives. Workers also develop strong preferences for technology. Too much variation in technology can reduce their productivity. Hence, the concept of "Bring Your Own Device" or BYOD has been gaining popularity recently. The concept is simple, but the variations in implementations in the name of cybersecurity is quite interesting.

The positive features of BYOD are many. Organizations can avoid the expense of providing and supporting a variety of mobile devices. They avoid the additional expense of upgrading to the latest and greatest model of these devices. Nor do they have to deal with the expense of replacing stolen or lost devices.

Users benefit also. They can select any device that suits their personal preferences and lifestyle. And most importantly, they only need to carry one device to keep up with their business and personal lives. On the surface, this sounds like a great proposition.

So how have organizations embraced BYOD? Essentially there are three camps:

1. Those who have chosen not to embrace it, citing security concerns;
2. Those who are embracing it, provided the BYOD owner will allow the organization to wipe all contents from the device in the event it feels there is a security risk; and
3. Those who are embracing it by creating a separate protected virtual environment called a "sandbox," which allows controlled entry into the organization's environment while keeping the user's personal environment separate and intact.

Given the democratization of technology and the ever-increasing market adoption of mobile devices, the first option is unlikely to be acceptable for very long.

The second option has four main issues:

1. It is not a very customer-friendly option.
2. It usually forces the user to choose an encrypted mode of operation, which will affect overall performance.
3. The risk of losing valuable data is extremely high for the user.
4. It is unlikely that the risk for the enterprise network will be properly mitigated.

In my opinion, the third option is the most promising. It allows an independent encrypted connection to the enterprise resources. At the end of the session, no data reside on the mobile device. This happy compromise should be acceptable to users as well as enterprise cybersecurity managers.

Most mobile device management (MDM) vendors already offer the "managed sandbox" capability with support for a wide range of mobile device operating systems. Remaining vendors are likely to offer this capability very soon in order to meet the market demand. Organizations can reduce costs and maintain better cybersecurity. What a great solution!

Using Modern Tools of Engagement

How do we encourage people to collaborate, share knowledge, and engage with others to solve large organizational issues and problems? This question was addressed directly and indirectly during several sessions at the 2012 Enterprise 2.0 conference in Boston. Enterprise 2.0 is the process of unleashing the collective brainpower of an organization and engaging everyone to innovate and contribute to its success.

Keynote speaker Bryan Barringer, manager of enterprise collaboration implementation at Fedex, provided valuable insight into this difficult problem in his presentation. Barringer shared the Fedex Badge Program, which is based on the concept of "gamification," in which desired employee behavior is encouraged by rewards of publicly visible badges of distinction.

As Barringer pointed out, unlocking enterprise knowledge has been difficult due to the traditional way of thinking that encouraged people to keep knowledge to themselves -- because this is what made them valuable. The gamified model redefines people's organizational value in terms of their ability to share and impart knowledge to others. It validates their contributions via distinctions bestowed by others in the organization. I am convinced that this could be the key to an enterprise collaboration strategy.

Even though we may not have been conscious of the process, gamification has already spurred people into competing for friends on Facebook, followers on Twitter, or connections on LinkedIn. In the enterprise, the same concept can be applied to motivate people to document and share knowledge, complete training, earn certifications, complete evaluations on time, present at conferences, write articles, mentor people, perform volunteer work, donate to causes, hire interns, answer questions posed by others, float new ideas, provide solutions to problems, or perform any other type of activity that an organization may desire. Gamification works better than retribution in an organization because it is a positive reinforcement.

So are our organizations ready for gamification? The answer may lie in an organization's ability to implement a new management model called Management 2.0. Presented by Chris Grams, David Mason, Nyla Reed, and Mary Woolf in a panel at the conference, this approach clarifies for me what is troubling about the management model prevalent in many organizations today -- adherence to hierarchy, top-down and one-way communications, rewards based on position rather than contribution, and leadership based on position rather than knowledge, skill, or ability. All of these approaches were designed for a bygone era.

As the panel elaborated on their 12 principles of Management 2.0, I realized that this new management model was powerfully grounded in social and collaborative principles that unleash the collective brainpower of an organization to drive innovation and success in an agile manner. This can be viewed as the new incarnation of the participatory style of management.

Andrew Carusone's presentation, "Beyond the Water Cooler: Using Collaborative Technology to Drive Business" shared an implementation of this model at Lowe's. Carusone pointed out that workforce development today was all about developing awareness, creating engagement, and promoting commitment. In his model, management continues to have decision and approval authority, but all employees have the power to recommend, provide input, and perform their duties to the best of their abilities.

Carusone also recommended a practical way to measure return on investment by counting things that are meaningful to the business, such as number of problems solved, customers gained, market share increased, employee retention rates, or other similar measures.

These sessions provided me the foundation to better understand the business need for and the powerful promise of enterprise social media technologies merging with traditional enterprise management technologies.

I had first attended Enterprise 2.0 in 2009. At that time, social media was being adopted in the enterprise as a fringe element by marketing and communications departments outside the purview and blessing of the IT department. Social media meant Facebook or Twitter, and many organizations blocked access to these sites. At the 2012 conference, it became clear to me that enterprise social media is becoming mainstream and much better understood at many major organizations. Text, audio, and video collaboration, along with gamification, are emerging as comprehensive enterprise management, collaboration, and productivity solutions. This phenomenon has now become so mainstream that elements of this conference is now present at most conferences and the need for a special Enterprise 2.0 conference appears to have waned.

Interoperable Videoconferencing Solutions

One of the modern tools of engagement is video conferencing. We have to be careful that we do not create "Video islands," or enterprise locations with internal, isolated videoconferencing facilities, which can cause interoperability challenges for collaboration. Within an island, communication and collaboration is easy, but it is difficult to communicate with people on other islands linked by the internet. Yet executive leaders have to focus on providing seamless connectivity between all types of video communications and conferencing solutions.

Three types of solutions, each offering high-quality audio and video, have emerged so far to address the issue.

Enterprise conference room solutions based on H.323 and related protocols come with sophisticated near and far camera controls. Investment can range from $20,000 to more than $100,000 per room. The solutions work great within the enterprise but can be challenging to use between organizations due to firewall rules. Cisco Systems and Polycom are two major vendors in this space.

Downloadable, user-friendly software-based person-to-person solutions by companies like Skype Ltd. and ooVoo have gained a large following by offering free calls worldwide. These solutions can traverse most firewalls (unless purposefully restricted).

Browser-based, user-friendly person-to-person solutions are available from players like Webex, GoToMeeting, AnyMeeting, and Google+. Cisco has rebranded Webex with social media features and called it Webex Social. A free Webex Basic is also available now.

The desire and need for interoperability among video islands is great. And when I met with several senior leaders recently, they all agreed on the following goals for enterprise videoconferencing equipment:

- Communication with a wide range of systems and platforms
- Easy communications through firewalls
- Easy authentication
- Easy-to-maintain features for contacts

- Access to directory services

With these goals in mind, is video interoperability possible? Though the technology is in its nascent state, there are a few glimmers of hope. Cloud vendors are providing solutions to this problem by writing interfaces that serve as a bridge between islands.

- Microsoft's Lync connects several types of video islands.
- Vidtel has tested interoperability between Skype, Google, Polycom, and Cisco.
- A Google+ enhancement can broadcast to unlimited users.
- Several H.323 clients such as ClearSea will connect PCs to enterprise systems, though they will require firewall rule changes.
- Internet2 members have an offering from SeeVogh.

Each solution has its limitations. However, due to the market opportunities and high demand, we are likely to see more innovative solutions in this rapidly evolving marketplace. Therefore, organizational leaders need to continuously seek better and highly interoperable solutions for video conferencing and collaboration.

Free and Open Source Software

Another expensive mistake that organizations make is to ignore open source and free software. Such software can work as well as or even better than commercial software. The most frequent reason I hear is: You will get better support if you buy the product. This line of thinking is seriously flawed. The strength of open source software is in its openness – anyone can examine the code and point out flaws and anyone can work on improving the product. There are more Linux servers in the world today than there are Windows servers.

Anti Virus and Anti Spyware for Windows

When I bought a new laptop recently, I noticed that a free one year subscription to a paid third-party anti-malware product was bundled into my purchase. As I spent time getting rid of the product along with various other unnecessary software that I never asked for, I started to wonder: Why are people still paying for anti-virus and anti-spyware solutions on Microsoft platforms?

A few years ago, Microsoft already solved this problem with their free Microsoft Security Essentials (MSE). I have used it happily on XP, Vista and Windows 7 and I know its functionality is incorporated into the Windows 8.x operating system. So why are PCs and laptops bundled with various other solutions? I wish I knew the answer.

Before MSE, IT professionals had their favorite anti-virus/anti-spyware solution and cleaning tools and it was difficult to avoid long never-ending debates over which one was the best. Now however, one would have to have a pretty convincing argument for not using MSE. Perhaps for a large enterprise with a need to manage every end-point, there may be an argument for a paid solution. However for the average home user or a small non-profit organization or a small business organization, MSE does the job very nicely – for free.

Once installed, it provides real-time protection from viruses and spyware, updates itself automatically and scans the machine off-hours or on demand. The program will automatically send Microsoft a report of the malware found and if a fix is available, it will get the latest fix to address the issue. The tool is configurable so users can change many of the settings and even turn some of the features off. So once again I ask: Why aren't more people using it? Is there some reason to use something else even though this is FREE?

Encryption

Ideally all laptops and thumb drives should be encrypted using a minimum AES 256 bit FIPS 140-2 compliant encryption to ensure that their loss does not pose a security/privacy risk. TrueCrypt is a free open source software which does an excellent job. TrueCrypt works on Windows 7/Vista/XP, Mac OS X, and Linux. TrueCrypt offers several types of encryption including the ability to encrypt an entire disk.

As far as TrueCrypt is concerned, all TrueCrypt containers are called Volumes and a Volume must be mounted on TrueCrypt before it can be accessed. TrueCrypt allows three common types of encryption: 1) Folder level encryption (which allows you to place several files into an encrypted container); 2) Disk level encryption (which allows you to encrypt your entire Windows volume); and 3) Device Level encryption (such as encrypting a thumb drive). You can even create a hidden encrypted folder.

It is best to visit the official TrueCrypt site http://www.truecrypt.org/ to download the software to ensure that you are not downloading an obsolete or fake version of the software.

Encrypted Zip

For people needing alternate solutions to zip a file and encrypt it with a simple password, JZip (www.jzip.com) provides a nice free solution.

Virtual Desktop Infrastructure (VDI)

VDI allows a single server to host many virtual desktop sessions, thus enabling any web-based machine to use a controlled desktop environment.

Enterprises implement VDI for the following main reasons:

1. Reduced cost
2. Better manageability
3. Enhanced security
4. Centralized license management
5. Ability to deploy browser-based thin clients

6. Worldwide access to enterprise applications with excellent performance.

While commercial solutions such as Citrix have been around for a while, the academic community has been deploying a free open-source solution called Virtual Computing Lab, developed at North Carolina State University (NCSU) for several years.

The solution was initially developed to solve the problem of providing students remote access to a virtual lab with the following goals in mind:

1. Eliminate the need to build expensive computing labs for students with high maintenance costs and only a single configuration on a given machine
2. Provide a dedicated compute environment for a limited time
3. Allow reservations to use an environment at a preferred time
4. World-wide access from any type of browser from any platform
5. Let faculty control the operating system type, version, patch level as well as all the loaded software in the environment
6. Ability for the user to perform anything within the virtual environment without affecting anyone else
7. Enable all users to get a fresh configuration at login
8. Centralized license management
9. Better security

The solution developed at NCSU addresses all these goals and much more remarkably well. Notice how similar these goals are to the VDI goals. It is a mature and well-supported product that has been deployed in many large academic institutions. The hardware deployed centrally in a VCL environment would be similar to the hardware needs of a VDI environment. However, VCL could be an excellent software alternative to a commercial VDI software for enterprises -- at a much lower cost. Check out how VCL works by visiting the NCSU website.

Organizations planning to implement VDI should take a look at the NCSU solution and evaluate if it would be an appropriate solution for them. The academic community is rich with many similar innovations, which could be applicable to the business environment.

Financial and Student Management Systems

The open-source Kuali Financial and Kuali Student Management Systems are excellent examples in this realm. Several major universities are involved in developing and implementing these major projects. It is best to talk to a few major universities to see how they have approached a particular problem. The additional information can help make a more comprehensive decision and save money. There could be a partnership opportunity with a local major university to even help build a solution. Granted, support for open-source can be challenging for many businesses -- this is another area where businesses should partner with a local major university to solve their business problems.

Word Processing, Spreadsheets, E-Mail, Calendaring, and Drive

The free word processing, spreadsheet, presentation, drawing, and database software Open Office (www.openoffice.org) has been around for many years and it keeps getting better and more powerful. It also gives the user the ability to open as well as create documents in Microsoft Office compatible formats.

Google has a complete multi-user solution of free applications which include, e-mail, word processing, spreadsheets, calendar, forms and other tools (apps.google.com). Their virus and spam control is exceptional. Google apps found under apps.google.com are multi-user – so multiple people can work on the same document at the same time in real time.

One of the most powerful free backup software available is Google Drive which automatically synchronizes a folder and all contents underneath the folder to Google Drive. It can be a life saver under many situations. In addition the files on the Google Drive can be available on the road from any computer.

Digital Libraries and YouTube

A very useful resource for people searching for scholarly work on any topic is scholar.google.com. The search will bring up books as well as journal articles with statistics on how many other people have cited a particular piece. This feature can help to identify the most important pieces of research very quickly.

YouTube is a great resource to learn how to do something and what other free resources might be out there.

In addition there are good free password management solutions, secure browser solutions and the list goes on and on. The world of free and open source software is rich with great solutions. People should exercise caution because there are fake sites, fake software and fake download tools which end up infecting machines. Then again there are many free clean-up tools also available. It is very important for executives and IT support personnel to make sure they help their employees by pointing out good free solutions.

Need for Multidisciplinary Focus in Education

In the new world of IT we need fewer programmers and more people with a multidisciplinary, holistic approach to information technology and cybersecurity. IT needs systems engineers and systems level thinkers.

Technology and information systems are now tightly integrated with every aspect of business. Organizations and business leaders today need to implement business IT systems that meet business requirements -- fast. IT is no longer about programming, database management, or office automation.

The new type of IT professional has leadership, communications, risk management, and project management skills to understand business requirements. This person can then visualize, propose, justify, and implement complex IT projects from beginning to end.

These technology professionals spend a lot of time developing a deep understanding of a business vertical, such as electronic transaction processing on the Web, healthcare, power plant control, chemical systems, spacecraft, or automotive engineering. Though we may call them IT professionals, they are more business professionals than they are technology professionals. They are strategic thinkers.

So where do we find these strategic thinkers? Most undergraduate university programs will not produce the interdisciplinary IT leaders that businesses need. Hence in many cases, these leaders are developed over time within the business environment. Of course, this is a slow and expensive process. In addition, due to the growing market demand and short supply, these people can be difficult to retain or replace.

The solution? Several academic institutions worldwide are putting together graduate programs in systems engineering and cybersecurity. The masters program in systems engineering at Cornell is a good example. It offers a flexible online format so that students can continue full-time employment while learning needed skills to advance their careers. The Cornell program also allows specialization within a business vertical.

In Maryland, Capitol Technology University has a high quality online master's and doctoral program in information assurance or cybersecurity. UMBC's Graduate School of Professional Studies offers a high quality master's degree in cybersecurity with on campus classes held in the evenings. All of these programs are geared towards full-time professionals and synchronous classes are held in the evenings.

In general, it is not easy to predict where an academic institution chooses to place such an interdisciplinary program. Should it be in the business school or the engineering school? Should it require some practical experience? A strong systems engineering program would require faculty collaboration from several disciplines.

Purely academic programs without opportunity to complete an actual project is likely to be less desirable than a program that combines academic training with practical experience. So some academic programs require practical project experience done in partnership within an industry of the student's choice. This is an excellent idea because many of the students who wish to go through a master's program of this type are already working for an organization that needs the skills of a systems engineer and will pay for the academic training.

Programs like the ones mentioned above can benefit from strong partnerships between academia, industry, and government. Several universities are creating opportunities to foster interdisciplinary collaboration among faculty, as well as to develop strong partnerships with industry and government.

This kind of model benefits everyone: Academic institutions gain additional revenue at low cost while extending their market well beyond their traditional geographic boundaries. Companies win the kinds of IT professionals they really need. Society benefits from better work in a range of industries. A win-win-win for everyone!

Technology Adoption in Higher Education

Technology and cybersecurity adoption is dramatically impacting many industries. I have always been intrigued by the promise of online education. It is easy to see how geographic and economic boundaries can be overcome through technology. Educational institutions can compete for students well beyond their traditional local boundaries, growing nationally and internationally while bringing down their per-seat costs. Schools no longer need expensive classrooms and dormitories to grow.

Small, innovative institutions can grow globally and as rapidly as they dare to dream. High-quality teaching faculty can be recruited from anywhere on the planet -- to teach thousands of students simultaneously. Students can study anytime and attend classes from anywhere. In addition, growth of free, high-quality education sites such as Khan Academy and open-source courses from MIT and others, along with global satellite and broadband communications networks, have removed economic, social, and geographic barriers to high-quality education.

However, several additional transformations are underway as well. Instead of printing expensive academic books, which quickly become obsolete, newer forms of interactive online books and educational and testing materials are being created. These books are not only easier to keep current, but they can also be brought to market rapidly at a much lower cost.

We can conduct literature reviews and browse the collections at several libraries (including Google Scholar) on any topic while sitting at our computers -- and we have a far richer experience than we would ever have had at a traditional library.

Libraries themselves are undergoing dramatic transformations. Instead of being quiet places with no food or drink allowed, they are becoming major hubs for collaboration, with cybercafés, conference facilities, multi-media rooms equipped with high-quality technology, and specialized digital collections.

Additionally, traditional student lab spaces are giving way to lower cost and flexible virtual labs, accessible anytime from anywhere, with hundreds of custom software configurations possible.

However, what has been most impressive to me, recently, has been not just the technology or the access, but a fundamental change in students' learning experience. Technology has brought people together in a more powerful way than ever before, similar to what social media did to global communications.

My fellow students in my doctoral classes at Capitol College were scattered all over the map geographically. We never met until a year into the program for our first residency. Yet we built an affinity and a relationship, and we could talk and discuss issues and ideas far more powerfully than I had ever experienced in a traditional classroom.

During class, we had audio and chat. Video was not enabled yet, though we have had video meetings and discussion sessions on Google+. The entire class session was recorded. We could use it for review or to attend asynchronously if we missed the class for some reason.

Class work was usually done in a collaborative manner. Since everyone in my class was a seasoned information technology professional, we had a lot to learn from each other. Our work papers and dissertation project ideas were posted for everyone else to comment on and critique in a helpful and constructive way, and we were graded on the quality of our suggestions to our peers.

We could review and comment on the work of others, at our own pace, anytime during a given week. Instead of receiving feedback from one professor, we receive high-quality feedback from 18 additional experts. We provided helpful references and knowledge based on our own expertise in the field. Our work product was refined in a dramatic way that simply would not have been possible in a traditional classroom.

More recently, while teaching for a university's online program, I experienced video enabled instruction with my students scattered all over the world. I sat in the comfort of my home while it snowed outside. Both audio and video were high quality and the interactions were excellent. Questions could be posted in chat. Students could raise their hands and speak or present as well. With no need to travel, the opportunity cost for attending for each student became dramatically low.

What a fabulous new world to learn in!

Technology for Doctoral Education

Given the promise of technology, we should always ask if it makes sense to continue doing things the way we've always done them. Surely it is time to redesign processes so that they take full advantage of the power now at our fingertips.

My first attempt at a doctoral degree was in political science at Emory University in the early 1980s. My department had a data lab with green and orange terminals connected to a couple of mainframe computers sitting on the other side of the campus. Word processing on the mainframes was possible with a bunch of cryptic commands on a line editor -- no spell or grammar check, and certainly no color or graphics. We had access to a dot matrix printer in the data lab for all our drafts. For good-quality printing, we had to queue jobs and then watch the queue to see if a job had printed. Then we walked or drove all the way to the other side of campus to get our outputs, which someone had placed neatly in bins. The first page had our IDs printed in big letters, so we could identify our papers.

Mansur Hasib working at the Emory University Data Center, Atlanta, Georgia – 1984

For statistics, we had access to mainframe versions of SPSS, SAS, and BMDP. To use them, we needed to know the cryptic Job Control

Language, which set up the job. These steps required tape numbers and tape mount commands, because the data we needed were on tapes, which technicians mounted for us. Every mistake or typo meant hours lost. Finding research articles or books meant manually flipping through card catalogues, taking out interlibrary loans, and weeks of waiting. Keyword search? No such thing. As a result, the typical doctoral program took 6-7 years to complete.

Fast forward to my more recent experience. Sitting in the comfort of my home, I had access to vast digital libraries with sophisticated author and keyword search. To help assess content quality, I could see the number of times others were using a piece of research. I downloaded and scanned article contents within minutes. Research that once took months now took minutes. I could visit multiple libraries virtually. On top of that, I had access to Google Scholar. Between the digital libraries and Google Scholar, I never needed to visit a library physically.

In the past, I might have used a phone or paper survey. This time I turned to free electronic surveys such as www.instant.ly, and I did not need to re-enter the data anywhere. I promoted and performed follow-ups to my survey using a wide variety of technologies, such as email and social media. I tracked responses in real-time, and high-quality color charts and crosstabs could be produced immediately. I could shut down the data collection the moment I had a representative sample. I downloaded the data and fed it into free statistical packages such as OpenStat by Bill Miller and Statistics Open for All (SOFA) by Paton-Sampson & Associates for further analysis. These programs also included high-quality color graphics.

A data collection and analysis effort that might have taken me six to twelve months previously was completed within a four-week timeframe. Incredibly, an entire project that could have taken six or seven years in the past was completely feasible within three years. Some students could finish even sooner -- if they could accelerate the work.

Technology at Public Schools

Technology is not only transforming the world of higher education, it is also creating a powerful sea change at schools world-wide – from elementary schools to high schools. I got a glimpse of this amazing technology-enabled future of worldwide collaboration in engineering after a relaxing visit with my college buddy and his family.

We visited the local robotics festival at South Orange Middle School in South Orange, New Jersey, with my friend and his sons, ages 8 and 10. I wasn't sure what to expect, but, as a technology enthusiast, I am always willing to learn what the next generation is thinking and doing with technology. This sure seemed like an interesting way to spend a lovely spring afternoon.

The show floor was packed with attendees and displays, including: JR First Lego teams (2nd and 3rd grade students), First Lego League (4th through 8th grade students), VEX Robotics (middle and high school students), and First Tech Challenge (high school students). Robot Revolution, which teaches elementary and middle school students to build and program real robots, was the sponsor.

I walked the show floor and admired the dexterity of these robots as young students controlled the motions using hand-held controls. The motions were quite complex and included picking up and dropping items. Lucas Ochoa, a sophomore at Livingston High School in Livingston, N.J., greeted me and asked if I had questions about his team's project.

Lucas enthusiastically explained the design of the various components of the robot that he and his teammate, fellow sophomore Menglong Guo, helped build. This robot had omni-directional motion enabled by Mechanum wheels and an innovative suspension system, which gives it far greater flexibility and traction compared to a traditional wheel and tire. Lucas also showed me design concepts behind each component on his smart phone.

Next-Generation Robotics

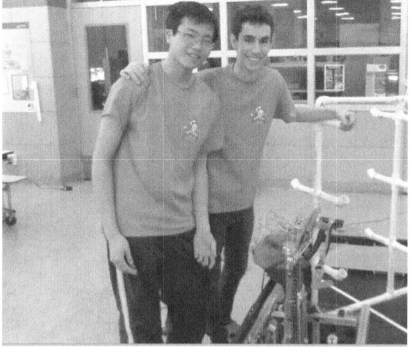

Menglong Guo (left) and Lucas Ochoa, sophomores at Livingston High School, during a robotics contest sponsored by Robot Revolution. South Orange, New Jersey - 2013

The materials used by the students are readily available online. Using video technology, students mentor other teams all over the world, Lucas said. And many of their robotics projects can be viewed at instructables.com. Check out the thermoelectric fan, powered by tealight candles.

Lucas and Menglong have been in training for two years, while their team (usually 10 members) has existed for about five years now. Their project and enthusiasm for building robots were impressive. I was also very impressed with their desire to help and mentor others -- what a great way to learn collaboratively with people all over the world. It made me feel highly optimistic about the future that these innovative citizens of the world will build, the startups they will create, or the organizations they will help empower.

Technology and Book Publishing

Closely tied to the world of education is the world of publishing. The publishing world has long been controlled by powerful companies with high costs, barriers to access, restrictions on distribution, one-sided copyright ownership contracts, and lengthy delays in getting critical information and knowledge out to a broad audience.

In this world, except for very famous authors who have some leverage, the remaining authors controlled little while publishers controlled everything. In the academic community, the sad result has been an excessive cost of textbooks. I had a first-hand taste of this during my recent doctoral work when even some black and white paperback cost almost $200! Technology is finally empowering authors.

I had been working as a free-lance writer for some online publications. When anything got accepted for publication, all I gave up was the initial right to publish for a period of 90 days. However the content and intellectual property always remained mine and after the initial period, I was free to do whatever I wanted with my work. So when an editor affiliated with a traditional publishing company asked me to contribute an article to a textbook, I expected something similar.

After I spent two weeks writing and rewriting the article to the editor's requirements, my article was approved. I then received a contract offer, which gave the publisher full ownership of all intellectual property rights permanently -- for the princely sum of $100. The contract offer also stipulated that I would be liable for breaches as well as "alleged breaches," and my work could be published without attribution to me. When I asked for a fair and balanced contract, the editor offered a take-it-or-leave-it option.

When I recently wanted to publish my doctoral dissertation and make it available at a reasonable cost to anyone in the world, I found all the traditional routes were skewed toward publishers. Some sites mentioned royalty payments, but nothing was clearly identified. Nowhere did I see any information about publishing timelines or how much control I would have.

My research led me to Kindle Direct Publishing and CreateSpace -- both Amazon companies. The entire process was quite transparent and I knew exactly how the royalty payments would work. Interestingly, royalty payments on the electronic platform were skewed completely in favor of the author. I had tremendous flexibility in pricing, plus the ability to change content, design covers, and the entire publishing process. In fact, I was able to publish the electronic version of my dissertation within 24 hours of my doctoral defense, and other doctoral students could buy it immediately at a very low cost.

The full color paperback version took more time because the template provided by CreateSpace was very difficult to work with. Still, I was able to do a respectable job in a week. CreateSpace provided everything necessary -- including the assignment of ISBN numbers -- and my book became available worldwide 10 days after my doctoral defense. Had I chosen to produce a black and white version, I could have priced it lower but it would have reduced quality since my work contains several pages of color charts.

Given a choice between color and black and white, it is best to choose black and white because the color version is at least twice as expensive. Once something has been published and sold in color, the same ISBN numbers cannot be used for a black and white version. An author can have a color as well as a black and white version of the same book.

The best part? My only expense was $25 to market my paperback to other bookstores and libraries. I could order copies of my book by paying CreateSpace's production costs, along with a shipping and handling fee. Within two weeks I saw other booksellers beginning to offer the item for sale. Kindle Direct Publishing lets me track sales in real time; CreateSpace has a time lag of several days. It was a very liberating and powerful experience. Recently, even this $25 cost has been eliminated.

For buyers of my paperback, I could offer a wide range of lower cost options to get the Kindle version. I could also offer it for free – so people could start reading immediately. The Kindle version does not require someone to own a Kindle. Instead, Amazon offers a Kindle eReader for almost all types of computer, tablet, or personal devices.

I can make changes to the interior of my books, and have the updates reflected within 24 hours. I can make changes whenever I feel they are needed. This is the future of publishing. It will reduce costs for consumers and allow authors to manage their content and pricing while retaining intellectual property rights and a fair share of royalties.

The CIO as President

I have often recommended that organizations should hire strategic CIOs as CEOs at their next opportunity. It is powerful when it happens. One of the most shining examples happened at a state-wide university system. In 1997, Indiana University (IU), which serves about 100,000 students on eight campuses, became one of the first academic institutions to elevate the job of CIO to a strategic position reporting to the president of the university. In 2007, IU made another notable decision by choosing a former CIO as its president.

What has followed is an example of how a president, a CIO, and other enterprise leaders can engage their community and propel it forward through technology powered strategic collaboration.

The Strategic Plan

Indiana University's president and its CIO now share a vision for the university. But they are not alone. The institution's strategic plan was developed with input from more than 140 representatives from across the university, as well as the University Information Technology Committee and the CIO's office. (Though the IT organization is centralized, individual campus needs are addressed by regional campus organizations headed by a campus CIO, who dual-reports to the campus chancellor and the central CIO.) In addition, the university conducts annual surveys to get input from students.

Instead of trying to lead in all areas of IT, IU aligned its strategic plan with university priorities and focused on a few key areas where it can excel and achieve distinction. The strategic plan has four key elements: Faculty and Scholarly Excellence, Student Success (which focuses on education and student living), Effective Community (which focuses on communication and collaboration within IU), and Engagement Beyond (which focuses on IU's mission in the state of Indiana and its standing and impact as an international university).

As part of that plan for IT, IU implemented a cyber infrastructure, which it defined as "computing systems, data storage systems, advanced instruments and data repositories, visualization environments, and people, all linked together by software and high performance networks to improve research productivity and enable breakthroughs not otherwise possible."

Specific Initiatives

To manage its financial and student systems at reduced cost, IU has been a key proponent of Kuali and other open-source initiatives. IU developed its own network operations and control software and uses it to manage gigapops in the region, bringing funding, jobs, and recognition to the IT department.

IUMobile is another major initiative, bringing the university's services to many mobile devices. IUPodcasts allow users to experience IU content in a rich multimedia format from anywhere in the world.

To encourage faculty to innovate in the use of technology, IU established a fund to support course or curriculum redesign, including rethinking how courses are taught, how technology can enhance the teaching and learning processes, and how classroom and learning space designs can support new teaching practices.

IU has created a technology-enabled virtual campus community, so its students can study, work, collaborate, and have fun. And it collaborates with many other academic institutions to share resources and produce academic cloud computing resources that benefit all. Sakai, Kuali Knowledge Management, EVIA, HathiTrust, and open-source grid computing environments are promising examples.

Additional helpful insight from the Indiana experience is available from an article written by president Michael McRobbie and CIO Brad Wheeler, "Three Insights for Presidents and CIOs," as well as a recent IU report, "Economic Engine for Indiana."

A Model for CEO/CIO Partnership in a City

I have always been quite impressed with Boston's use of video technology and social media to fight crime. Boston was among the first US cities to use robot technology to examine sewers. I found out the reason behind the innovations when I attended a session where Laurianne McLaughlin, editor-in-chief of InformationWeek.com interviewed Bill Oates, CIO of the City of Boston.

I learned that in 2005, Mayor Thomas Menino recognized the importance of technology and innovation for Boston's future, and made the CIO a cabinet position reporting directly to the mayor. He also created an office of innovation and located it right next to the Mayor's office. Thus Boston became one of the earliest cities to make strategic use of a CIO.

One of the most successful projects in building a better relationship with citizens has been Citizens Connect, which replaced the old hotline. While the old hotline had been a complaint mechanism, citizens using the new system feel like they are helping with solutions. This led to a whole new demographic of people joining.

To encourage even more citizen participation, the city used gamification to recognize citizens when they reported potholes. Citizens notice when the potholes they reported are fixed and post pictures -- resulting in an excellent engagement experience. These innovations in Boston are being emulated elsewhere. Named Commonwealth Connect, the system now being built in Massachusetts will initially include 46 communities and represent about 38 percent of the state population.

Boston also became one of the earliest cities to use robots to examine their vast networks of sewer pipes. Apparently the technology has been around for a while and it does more than examining. RedZone Robotics redesigned robots originally created to examine dangerous places, such as high nuclear radiation areas to examine sewers, both above water level and below.

By using robots instead of people, Peachtree City, North Carolina checked all collection pipes in 15 months. Checking all these pipes with crews would have taken the city's utility about 15 years. The robots cost about $178,000 annually for seven years, comparable to the cost of the smaller-scale manual testing.

Collaboration between city, industry and academia resulted in the creation of Medrobotics. This company makes robots which crawl into the vasculature of humans to examine medical issues, thus avoiding expensive invasive surgery and even making impossible examinations possible.

From sewers to potholes to vascular veins, businesses and government agencies should look to their neighbors for inspiration. We can learn a lot from each other if we stop, talk, and listen.

A Model for CEO/CIO Partnership in Healthcare

By far the best story I heard at the 2013 World Health Congress event was the amazing CEO/CIO partnership at Kaiser Permanente (KP). This partnership between CEO George Halvorson and CIO Phil Fasano shows how technology, data, and analytics powers the organizational strategy and mission of Kaiser Permanente, enabling this healthcare organization to become a model for others to emulate.

The non-profit health plan has 9 million plan members, and delivers services in nine states, as well as in Washington, D.C. Innovation and continuous improvement through use of technology and data are the organizational culture at KP, said Halvorson. "We want to be the best at getting better," he said.

To accomplish that, KP came up with "four pillars of excellence" to build upon. They include:

1. Big Q, which is the governance framework that engages KP's top executives in the quality and data initiative.
2. Electronic Medical Library and Support Tools, which provide access to a rich repository of medical books and journals, and are used extensively by 300,000 users per month.
3. Care Management Institute, where 138 full-time professionals read journals, review research, and ensure that the medical technology infrastructure is continuously maintained at the state of the art level.
4. Innovation Centers that are actively engaged in fostering and promoting the culture with quality and safety competitions at an international scale.

KP's approach to innovation is similar to that of Tata Steel, an approach which helped power Tata to greatness in the late 1980s. That concept rests on the fact that people who do nothing never fail. And if you try 10 new things, a couple of them will fail -- but that failure is learning by itself. In similar vein, Fasano explained, "We want to fail early and fail cheap."

Fasano also explained how KP uses the strategic information assurance of maximizing confidentiality, integrity, and availability of information and systems. Their goal is also to ensure that systems are intuitive and easy to use. Technology has allowed doctors to see more members and provide far better care than would otherwise be possible.

KP Senior VP and COO, Hal Wolf, provided a glimpse into how KP is engaging patients with their portal called My Health Manager, which, in 2012, had 4.1 million users -- representing nearly half of KP members. This portal allows patients to schedule appointments, view lab results, and has many other member wellness-focused features. Users can access the portal via a wide range of mobile platforms.

In fact, the healthcare improvement and cost reduction goals of the Affordable Care Act were modeled after the KP experience, Halvorson said.

The KP experience and the financial impact of technology, electronic tools, and data mining, are chronicled in two newly published books: *KP Inside*, by George C. Halvorson, and *Transforming Healthcare*, by Philip Fasano.

Technology Adoption in Healthcare

The pace of technology adoption in healthcare has been accelerating following the passage of the Health Information Technology for Economic and Clinical Health (HITECH) Act of 2009, helped along by the dramatic democratization of access to technology, and then the passage of the Affordable Care Act in 2010.

Paper patient records are giving way to electronic health records (EHR). Paper prescriptions are giving way to e-prescriptions, whereby the doctor directly sends the prescription order electronically to be filled or refilled by the patient's choice of pharmacy. The patient then simply shows up at the pharmacy to pick it up. Video, e-mail, and social media technology are allowing improved access to doctors, with patients able to rate their experiences.

Doctors and nurses are increasingly using tablets and other handheld devices to manage patient visits. Patients are able to view their health information and make and change appointments online using their own computers, tablets, or other handheld devices. It is anticipated that by 2015 100% of doctors and nurses will be using mobile devices as their primary device. Technology is being used to monitor patient status and provide patients with discharge instructions and reminders about how and when to take their medications.

Major EHR vendors are building Health Information Exchanges (HIE) to allow care providers to exchange patient information and access a complete picture of a patient's health in order to provide better care. Major hospitals are signing up with vendors to participate in these exchanges.

To make it easy for doctors to adopt technology into their practices, several options are available. Many doctors simply sign up with a free EHR provider, which eliminates the need to hire and manage technology staff or maintain servers. The major disadvantage is that the doctor has to plan for a possible service outage, which is frequently mitigated by requiring the provider to maintain a local copy of the data. The other disadvantage is that the service provider may sell de-identified patient data for research purposes (something that HIPAA allows).

Other options include hiring a managed services organization (MSO) to provide hosting and management services or to facilitate a transition for the doctor's practice into a third-party managed service. Eligible doctors, hospitals, and care providers can recoup expenses of migrating to an EHR by filing for Meaningful Use incentive payments.

Maryland recently became the first state to connect all of its hospitals to a health information exchange (HIE). Maryland's HIE is a mechanism for transport, connection, and exchange of medical information. This system does not store patient data. Patients are opted in by default but can opt out of the system if they wish.

In 2009, Maryland also adopted rules to allow doctors to practice telemedicine, and legislative bills that would allow doctors to be reimbursed by insurers for telemedicine visits are underway. Maryland also received a grant to build a health *insurance* exchange.

During the Supreme Court deliberations, the big question was: What happens if the federal healthcare law is overturned by the Supreme Court? If this had happened, chances are high that efforts in some states would have continued unabated -- though funding could have become challenging.

In other states, such as Maryland, where the state law refers to the federal law instead of incorporating its provisions into the state law as some states did, overturning the federal law would most likely have overturned the state law as well. Thus a period of confusion and uncertainty would have persisted. However, the genie is out of the bottle!

A Firsthand Experience of Healthcare IT

With everything that was going in healthcare, I was very curious to learn what my own doctor was doing. So in early 2011, when I visited my doctor, I was giddy with anticipation. When I walked up and announced myself at the reception desk, the attendant handed me an orange-colored rugged, touch screen tablet PC and asked me to sign in.

After logging in, I was surprised to find all of my billing information already lined up. I was able to update my insurance information, sign my releases and HIPAA forms, all within minutes. I did not have to fill out any of those dreaded paper forms on a clip board!

Once in the doctor's office, I noticed a change as well. Though the doctor still had a manila folder with my blood pressure readings from past visits, he was also using a desktop PC with a 22-inch screen, which appeared to have all my records.

"So, you've converted to electronic health records?" I asked the doctor.

"Yes," he grinned. "But it's expensive and I'm not sure I like it."

"But you are getting incentive payments, right? Meaningful Use credits... You are applying for that, aren't you?"

"Meaningless Use," he laughed. "They really didn't think this through. The things they are asking us to report on are meaningless."

"Did you connect to the health information exchange?" I pursued, "You know, Maryland has already connected all hospitals to the health information exchange. You can also practice telemedicine and get reimbursed for that now."

"Oh, I didn't know that," the doctor replied. "Although I'm not sure that I could check a patient's symptoms through a Webcam."

"Perhaps not, but some things could be done through telemedicine. Anyhow, Maryland is also building a health insurance exchange."

Before I could finish, the doctor perked up. "You mean anyone can buy health insurance through the exchange?"

"Yes," I said. "And if someone wants to become a consultant or loses a job, they don't have to lose health insurance."

"Now that would really be helpful," the doctor added thoughtfully. "I know several patients who would be able to get back into the workforce if they could get treatment for their illnesses, which are preventing them from working. It's a vicious cycle -- they cannot work because of their illness and because of that they cannot get health insurance and proper treatment. They have been to several insurance companies who will only insure them if they can exclude paying for the illness they have, so they remain sick and cannot get back into the workforce. The insurance exchange will really help people."

The doctor and I were almost finished with our visit. He took out his pad to write me a prescription. "Don't you use e-prescriptions?" I asked, puzzled.

"Yes, I do."

"Then order in my prescription through e-prescription. Don't you like being able to just order in a prescription?"

"Yes, that I do like. But sometimes it doesn't go through. If you go to the pharmacy and expect to pick up the medicine right now, it may work better to have that piece of paper in hand," the doctor warned.

"Well no, I will just visit there or call in to make sure they got it. I can wait to pick it up tomorrow," I volunteered.

As a technology person, I resolved to let technology work for me. The doctor asked me which pharmacy I wanted to use, and I watched him make a few clicks. It did not even take two seconds before he got up with a smile and said, "Okay, it's done."

It was a short, 10-minute drive to the pharmacy. I walked up to the counter excitedly and asked if my e-prescription had been received. The pharmacist asked for my birthday and then my name. I volunteered my prescription card. She squinted at the screen through her glasses.

"Did my prescription come in?" I asked.

"Yes," she nodded as she squinted closer at the screen after waiting what seemed like an eternity to me.

"When can I pick it up?" I asked.

She squinted some more. "Let me see where it is," she replied finally and went around to the bin and picked out an envelope. "Come around to the other side and get in line," she said.

"You mean it's ready? I can pick it up now? Wow, I love this new world of technology-powered healthcare!"

And thus ended my first visit to the doctor in a technology-powered healthcare world. Although I was excited, I realized there were many things that needed to happen to make things work right.

Cybersecurity Leadership in Healthcare

My national study in healthcare in 2013 (Hasib, 2013) found that nearly half of the CIOs in the US healthcare sector do not report to the CEO. In addition, as shown in the chart below, one out of five US healthcare organizations do not plan to hire a CISO anytime soon.

4. Does your organization have a position with a role and title equivalent to a Chief Information Security Officer?

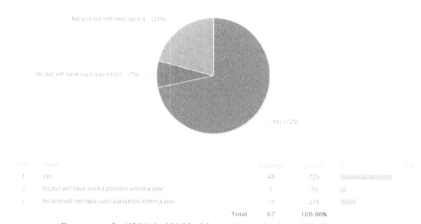

	Answer		Responses	Percent		
1	Yes		48	72%		
2	No but will have such a position within a year		5	7%		
3	No and will not have such a position within a year		14	21%		
		Total	67	100.00%		

Presence of a CISO in US Healthcare Organizations (Hasib, 2013)

The advent of health information technology is a very recent phenomenon. In addition, the legal landscape for healthcare is changing and evolving rapidly making it very challenging for healthcare organizations. In recent months, the industry has also suffered from several sensational breaches. The need for cybersecurity leadership in healthcare is more critical now than ever before. Ethics and integrity are at the forefront of this critical need (Sorrell, 2012).

I was curious to learn why healthcare organizations were not planning to hire a CISO. I wondered if the reporting level or empowerment of the CIO in the organization had an impact on this condition. I thought that organizations where the CIO reported to the CEO were more likely to have a CISO. However, as the following chart shows, the data did not support this hypothesis.

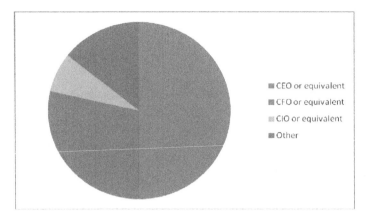

CEO or equivalent
CFO or equivalent
CIO or equivalent
Other

Reporting Relationship of US Healthcare CIOs with No Plans for CISO within a Year

Half of the organizations with no plans for a CISO were organizations where the CIO reported to the CEO or equivalent officer. This led me to conclude that CIO empowerment does not determine the level of importance placed on cybersecurity.

Implications of Healthcare Legislation

The Health Insurance Portability and Accountability Act of 1996 (HIPAA) established the initial information security and privacy standards for the healthcare industry. The law also established Protected Health Information (PHI). Simply stated, PHI are patient data whose confidentiality is legally protected. The law created obligations for organizations which stored, transmitted, and exchanged such data.

However, until 2009, there was no enforcement mechanism or audit processes. For many healthcare providers, implementation of HIPAA simply meant they had to get patients to sign a form. Poor habits of handling and discussing PHI carelessly has therefore become ingrained in the healthcare sector.

The Health Information Technology for Economic and Clinical Health (HITECH) Act of 2009 attempted to address these problems by requiring breach notifications, by establishing penalties, and by specifying enforcement procedures. HIPAA audits started in 2011. The other key requirement was the implementation of electronic health records (EHRs) and related health information technology (HIT).

These changes require the healthcare industry to adopt health information technology and cybersecurity. The law requires mandatory encryption of protected health information in storage and during transmission. It also establishes significant fines for non-compliance. New rules also establish significant personal and perpetual liability for workers responsible for breaches.

Under the new rules, members of the public have several key rights:

- *Individual access* – people must be given easy access to view their information.
- *Correction* – people must be allowed to request correction of their information in a timely manner.
- *Openness and transparency* – people have the right to know who has access, and how the information will be stored, used and shared.
- *Individual choice* – people must be provided choice to make informed decisions about the collection, use, and disclosure of their protected information.
- *Collection, use, and disclosure limitations* – organizations have to create, collect, and use protected information only to the extent necessary to provide service and never to discriminate inappropriately.
- *Data quality and integrity* -- organizations must ensure that protected information is complete, accurate, and up-to-date to the extent necessary for service and has not been altered or destroyed in an unauthorized manner.
- *Safeguards* – organizations must protect the legally protected information with reasonable operational, administrative, technical, and physical safeguards to ensure its confidentiality, integrity, and availability and to prevent unauthorized or inappropriate access, use, or disclosure.
- *Accountability* – organizations must implement these principles, monitor adherence, take prompt action with any cases of non-adherence, and promptly report large scale breaches to both the individuals involved and to the Department of Health and Human Services.

HIEs are health information exchange highways at the state level to connect all healthcare providers in the state and to allow seamless and secure exchange of patient information so that complete and accurate patient information is available to healthcare providers. Such exchange and access to information would reduce errors, obviate expensive and redundant tests, and ultimately result in lowered costs and better care. The

HIEs were also meant to provide patients with the ability to view their information and seek rectification of errors in a timely manner. They could also opt out of agreeing to allow exchange of their information.

Since 2010, significant work on state HIEs has been done as a result of financial incentives authorized by the HITECH Act of 2009. Thirty-four states and the District of Columbia received first-round funding to build HIEs. Some states such as Delaware and Maryland successfully connected all hospitals and progressed to the second stage of funding for operations, but some early innovator states actually returned the federal money and held back work on the exchanges.

To assist organizations with the expenditures related to the implementation of HIT and information security, HITECH provided substantial financial incentives to healthcare providers who adopted HIT and cybersecurity through the Meaningful Use EHR Incentive Program.

The Affordable Care Act of 2010, required the establishment of health insurance exchanges at the state level. Health insurance exchanges (HIX) are designed to allow anyone to compare health insurance options and to buy health insurance. These marketplaces allow insurance companies of any size to offer services and compete without having to have a massive technology infrastructure. The concept is very similar to an electronic securities trading exchange, which democratized stock trading and allowed small investors and individuals to get quotes and to buy stocks and other securities at low trading fees.

The law also provides transparency in prices and coverage. It requires a basic minimum level of coverage and also guarantees that insurance cannot be terminated when someone falls ill. There can be no discrimination based on gender or pre-existing conditions. Lifetime caps on insurance have also been eliminated. Therefore consumers actually know up front what is their maximum possible annual out-of-pocket expense in healthcare. Annual checkups were also included as a free service.

The law also provides for the establishment of healthcare savings accounts (HSA). These accounts allow people to save pre-tax dollars each year for healthcare expenses. The money in these accounts carries forward from year to year. People can accumulate and invest the money just like a 401K retirement account. HSA funds can be used to buy most over the counter medicines, prescription glasses and other healthcare related products and services. Tax advantages of an HSA are similar to retirement accounts.

In order to prevent health insurance companies from having a profit incentive to deny healthcare benefits, a key provision of the law is the requirement for insurance companies to spend 80% of the money collected on actual healthcare. The law provides significant freedom to states to certify insurance company policies and to help regulate rates. Individuals who do not qualify for tax rebates can also go directly to a health insurance provider and purchase a policy of their choice. They do not have to fear that the policy will be inferior or be more expensive because these policies have to meet minimum standards and be the same price as the same policy being sold on the health insurance exchange.

HIXes had to be functional in states by 2014, and states had to make their intentions known by Dec. 14, 2012. Many states embraced the law, obtained the financial incentives to build the HIX, and got on schedule to open a health insurance exchange on October 1, 2013. Several states received funding to build state-run HIXes. Some states exchanges such as Kentucky and Connecticut have been very successful. Other states such as Maryland and Oregon had serious problems.

Many states could not build these exchanges because bills to establish these exchanges failed in their state legislatures. The federal government had to build exchanges for states which did not build their own health insurance exchanges. This created an extraordinary burden on the federal project to build www.healthcare.gov.

An important new requirement which health insurance exchanges had to contend with was the handling of Federal Tax Information (FTI). FTI is defined as confidential non-public information that individuals filed in their tax returns and amendments to the Internal Revenue Service (IRS). IRS Publication 1075 contains the details on criminal and civil penalties for violations.

As an example, there is a penalty of $1000 and/or up to 1 year imprisonment, plus costs of prosecution for willful unauthorized access of a return information. Willful unauthorized disclosure of a return has a penalty of $5000 and/or up to 5 years imprisonment, plus costs of prosecution (Internal Revenue Service, 2014).

These penalties are for individuals working on health insurance exchanges. Their perpetual obligation to protect survives separation from their jobs. Workers handling FTI must also undergo training, sign forms, keep detailed records, and maintain logs of receipt and disposal. They must access strictly on a need to know basis.

The Roll-Out of Health Information Exchanges in the USA

When health insurance exchanges opened on October 1, 2013 I perused the sites of every state and noted something very interesting: As the following table shows, although the government runs all these health insurance exchanges (HIXs), not all reside on .gov sites. Excluding the federal site and a handful of state sites, the rest dwell on .com or .org websites. I found this quite surprising -- and alarming.

STATE BRANDED EXCHANGES	WEBSITE	BRAND NAME
California	www.coveredca.com	Covered California
Colorado	http://connectforhealthco.com/	Connect for Health Colorado
Connecticut	https://www.accesshealthct.com	Access Health Connecticut
District of Columbia	https://dchealthlink.com/	DC Health Link
Hawaii	http://www.hawaiihealthconnector.com/	Hawaii Health Connector
Idaho	http://www.yourhealthidaho.org/	Your Health Idaho*
Kentucky	https://kyenroll.ky.gov/	KYNECT
Maryland	http://www.marylandhealthconnection.gov/	Maryland Health Connection
Massachusetts	https://www.mahealthconnector.org/	Massachusetts Health Connector
Minnesota	http://www.mnsure.org/	MNSure
Nevada	https://www.nevadahealthlink.com	Nevada Health Link
New Mexico	https://bewellnm.com/	BeWell*
New York	http://healthbenefitexchange.ny.gov/	New York State of Health
Oregon	http://www.coveroregon.com/	Cover Oregon
Rhode Island	http://www.healthsourceri.com/	Health Source RI
Utah	http://www.avenueh.com/	Avenue H
Vermont	http://healthconnect.vermont.gov/	Health Connect Vermont
Washington	http://www.wahealthplanfinder.org/	Washington Health Plan Finder
	-	*Sends to Federal Site

PARTNERSHIP EXCHANGES	-	
	-	
Arkansas	www.healthcare.gov	
Delaware	www.healthcare.gov	
Illinois	www.healthcare.gov	
Iowa	www.healthcare.gov	
Michigan	www.healthcare.gov	
New Hampshire	www.healthcare.gov	
West Virginia	www.healthcare.gov	
	-	
FEDERAL MARKETPLACE		
Federal Marketplace	www.healthcare.gov	

For marketing purposes, each state chose a catchy brand name. While many of these brand names are quite memorable and suitable for strong branding with their target market, I think every site should have used a .gov domain name. This would have made it easier for members of the public to recognize real websites and not fall prey to fake website scams.

The General Services Administration (GSA) -- a division of the federal government -- registers .gov domain names. Commercial domain registration organizations register .org and .com websites. Thus registering a fake .com and .org health insurance website is far easier than registering a fake .gov website.

This particular oversight has created confusion already and is likely to create more confusion. Worse, it will cause many innocent people to become victims of a scam. Fake websites also can provide a lot of false and misleading information. Agencies should fix this immediately before fake and competing health insurance websites pop up and cause damage all over the country. The official state and federal sites should always be .gov sites.

Why the Federal Site and Several State Sites Stumbled

While analyzing the publicly available information on the problems with the federal and states sites, it was clear to me that the failures were mostly on the executive leadership and project management side. These projects were being run by healthcare executives instead of being run by technology and cybersecurity executives. The healthcare executives were constantly overruling the IT executives and even adding complex functional requirements which were completely unnecessary for initial operation.

All projects have three key dimensions called constraints: schedule, scope, resources. Since the schedule of the health insurance exchange projects was not negotiable, either scope had to be constrained to meet the schedule or adequate resources had to be added. In these projects the scope should have been carefully trimmed to only what was needed to be successful. No scope creep should have been allowed. Additional functionality should have been put on a future schedule.

Another problem was an unrealistic setting of expectations and everyone's failure to realize that innovation inherently carries with it some risk -- and, hence, the potential for gain. Most innovation requires tweaking and adjustment based upon actual field testing. If major companies like Microsoft, Google, and Facebook -- and even simpler college application systems or job application systems -- require several iterations before becoming reasonably stable and reliable, why do we expect complex, sophisticated, multi-layered health insurance exchanges to have a smoother release? Even after a release is "stable," doesn't Microsoft continue to send out weekly patches?

The signup requirement before being able to browse plans was another unnecessary burden to the system. Additionally, there were too many single choke points in the system. For example, every state sign-up process required the state system to query the federal site electronically to verify information such as legal status, address, income, family information and many other pieces of information. Clearly this traffic and workload could have been geographically dispersed throughout the US. Even account creation and other functions could have been spread out geographically but were not.

The public were not engaged and informed properly and there was so much fear of electronic health records in the minds of people that many chose a manual sign-up or a manual verification or both. This caused substantial delays for these people in getting their insurance applications approved.

The Need for Healthcare Communities and Patient Engagement

There has been a lot of discussions about the need for more engagement of members of the public in the discussions of healthcare. It is also one of the requirements of the Meaningful Use provisions of the HITECH Act.

Healthcare providers are building portals to provide such engagement. However, these solutions are creating portal islands -- each with its own requirement to authenticate -- each providing only a sliver of information. The public needs to go to a single place for all their information – a single location which could be their gateway to all the various portals.

Kaiser Permanente's community and public engagement portal has been very successful. But many others suffer from spotty adoption and low market penetration. The debut of www.healthcare.gov and the various states exchanges could have tried to solve this problem by using Enterprise 2.0 and Web 2.0 technologies to build healthcare communities instead of static one way web-sites. This should be attempted in future iterations.

Communities would allow everyone to participate in the building of content and to engage in meaningful conversations. It is interesting to note that on the very same day that the federal site went live, another site (albeit a far less complex one) proved to be very successful: www.msnbc.com. This site is definitely a Web 2.0 site, encouraging a relationship with people, and promoting conversations and participation. It allows participants to create their own affinity group, start new discussion threads, and share links, all with the usual features of allowing comments, additional sharing, liking, and lots of other bells and whistles.

Here are a few salient reasons why states (and even federal) organizations should create Web 2.0 healthcare websites:

1. There are many natural affinity groups that need to share information with each other as well as members of the public: healthcare providers, doctors, nurses, health aides, insurers, brokers (now called producers), navigators, assisters (people who help the public in signing up for healthcare coverage), and case workers (members of local health departments or state departments of human resources).
2. Most current state websites do not change content enough to encourage people to visit them regularly. You cannot create brand recognition or an affinity to a website without being a vibrant and active site.
3. It is far better to have several thousand people contribute to your content than a few anointed official webmasters. The old Web 1.0 model does not work anymore for brand promotion and engagement of a target audience.

4. Due to the scale of the changes happening in this area, people have too much misinformation, apprehension, and confusion. Without the ability to properly express, discuss, and resolve such confusion, the associated stress will continue.
5. Crowd sourced responses and discussions tend to be timely, rapid, and more comprehensive.
6. People have real stories to share. Regardless of the nature of the story -- positive or negative -- these tales are highly likely to help others, as well as the people sharing the stories.
7. All healthcare related information sessions and local town halls can be archived and be made available on these sites, creating a longer lasting impact and outreach for these sessions.
8. If these town halls and information sessions are simulcast on the website, more people can attend.
9. People would be able to participate in opinion polls on various topics of the day.
10. Since people will have to sign up to participate on the websites, there will be an established base of people to communicate with regularly to get reactions and opinions on new ideas and improvements.
11. It will reduce unmoderated discussions on other social platforms.

The Vision for a National Health Information Network

Though people are passionately discussing health information exchanges and health insurance exchanges today, and it has become a highly politicized issued, it is important to recognize that the vision for all Americans to have access to electronic health records (EHRs) by 2014 began in 2004 -- as a very bipartisan vision for progress.

At that time, President George W. Bush established the position of National Coordinator for Health Information Technology within the Department of Health and Human Services and laid the foundation for a Nationwide Health Information Network (NHIN). The goals of the NHIN are seamless connectivity and secure exchange of healthcare information nationwide. It is neither a national network nor a bunch of servers run by the federal government. Instead, it is a set of standards and tools developed by a core group with significant experience in building health information exchanges.

Federal agencies such as the Department of Defense, the Centers for Disease Control, the Veterans Administration, and the Social Security

Administration; states such as Delaware (home to the nation's first statewide health information network), New York, North Carolina, Virginia, and West Virginia; educational institutions such as Indiana University and Wright State University; and private healthcare organizations such as Kaiser Permanente and the Cleveland Clinic were among the initial participants in the NHIN.

Technology to build HIEs, initially developed by federal agencies, was released to the public domain in the form of CONNECT, a free, open-source software solution that lets anyone build HIEs and connect to the NHIN. An organization can build an HIE to communicate between internal EHR systems, join an HIE, or communicate with EHR systems of other organizations.

The Human Factor in Healthcare

In the healthcare industry, 80-90% of the data security breaches between 2008 and 2010 happened through insiders (HIMSS Analytics, 2010). My own survey in 2013 found that nearly 80% of the responders had insider related incidents (Hasib, 2013). Insiders are defined as employees or affiliated and contractual personnel who have legitimate access to information (Probst, Hunker, Goleman & Bishop, 2010). Thus a focus on people controls and cybersecurity leadership by a healthcare executive such as chief information officer will have a major influence in guaranteeing the safety of protected information used by teams in healthcare.

Such controls are typically applied through policy, contracts, training, and through leadership and management techniques which promote a cybersecurity culture. Executives in healthcare can use cybersecurity leadership, team building, employee engagement and other leadership and ethical concepts to build a cybersecurity culture which secures information used by physicians, nurses, medical professionals/technicians, or other healthcare workers.

Of course, the typical controls such as data classification, authorization, encryption, data obfuscation (which breaks up files into pieces residing at multiple locations), multi-factor authentication, auditing, monitoring, logging and other routine, physical and widely accepted information security layers have to be present. After that we need to systematically develop a cybersecurity culture as outlined in this book. The following are some nuanced recommendations for the healthcare sector:

- *Values* -- In healthcare organizations patient safety is already a value. It would be easy to connect patient data safety to this value.
- *Policy and Contractual Controls* -- Executives should adopt organization policies which clearly embrace the organizational values and identify appropriate use and safeguards for protected information. Each person who has access to such information should be required to acknowledge that they have read and understood the policy. Each person should be required to sign perpetual non-disclosure agreements.

  These agreements should clearly require the non-disclosure obligations to perpetuate perennially even after disassociation from the organization. There should be contracts with all related organizations with regard to mutual safety obligations related to proprietary and confidential information. It should be obvious to everyone that these documents and controls are extensions and instruments of the organizational values.
- *Data Classification* -- The data should be classified in accordance with its sensitivity. There should be a conscious documentation of who needs access to what information. Proper records should be maintained on the authorization of this access. There should be a proper change management process for changes to access controls. The teams should be fully aware of the sensitivity of the data they use. They should know who has access to what type of information. They should be vigilant in ensuring that everyone uses the information and access in a responsible and intended manner.
- *Auditing* -- There should be policies and procedures to track when information is retrieved, by whom and when it is securely returned to its place of rest. Departures of any member should be governed by policies and procedures which remove access from people who are no longer within the team. Access could be time controlled as well as geographically restricted. Data could be prohibited from being moved, copied or carried away in an unauthorized manner. Controls and expenditures of resources need to be proportionate to the sensitivity and risk associated with the information.
- *Code of Ethics* – An easily understood, accepted, and practiced code of ethics should be implemented throughout the organization by all employees, contractors and partners who are working closely with the organization and handling protected information.

Leaders Developing Leaders

A layered leadership model should be implemented. Everyone should be trained on how to be a catalyst leader so they can nurture and create other leaders and lead through an adoption of personal and organizational values. Everyone should have the ability and freedom to question unsafe actions by anyone. There should be a culture that promotes active constructive confrontation and immediate correction of any unsafe action by any member of the organization.

People attempting to improve the safety of the organization should have immunity from all types of retribution. People, who are unwilling to adopt the culture of the organization and live its values, should be carefully culled. Left unchecked, such detractors will have a devastating effect on the safety and security of the teams and the organization as a whole.

Each team member should be trained on what a team is. They should understand the difference between a group and a team. They should understand that they have a shared mission and collective responsibility. They should share insights, information and perspectives. Their decisions should support the collective mission of the team and allow each individual to perform his or her job better. There should be a sense of interdependence and appreciation for complementary and diverse skills within the team.

Team members should be encouraged to contribute to decisions and should feel empowered to make appropriate decisions with full awareness of the extent of their authority. They should know when they may need to consult some other member of the team for some decision. They should know how to plan and prepare for absences and team membership changes. Each team member should feel valued and important within the team and know how they are positively impacting the mission of the team and the organization. Of course the role of healthcare executives in making the right things happen will be very important. We have a dramatic opportunity in front of us to do the right thing for the healthcare of our people.

The Future of Health Information Technology

Electronic health records (EHRs) are the cornerstone of improving healthcare and reducing costs. To participate in health information exchanges (HIEs) and to qualify for federal Meaningful Use incentive payments, eligible healthcare practitioners must adopt EHR systems certified by the Office of the National Coordinator (ONC).

Large hospitals, academic medical centers, and healthcare organizations have the scale, finances and personnel needed to implement fairly expensive EHR solutions from vendors like Epic, Cerner, GE Centricity, Allscripts, and Meditech. These systems also require a lengthy implementation schedule. Providers typically need internal and contractual staff not only for implementation and integration but also for maintaining these systems. Small, individual medical practices and even some midsized facilities, however, can neither afford to implement nor maintain such systems on their own. What are their options? Fortunately, there are some low cost choices.

Free EHRs

Providers can sign up with a free certified cloud-based EHR system from a developer such as www.practicefusion.com or www.hellohealth.com. Both solutions allow a doctor's office to adopt an EHR quickly, and both have powerful features with extensive customization options to suit the needs of doctors and patients.

Practice Fusion is trying to be the Google of the healthcare world with a fully cost-free model for doctors. One way the company makes money is by selling deidentified patient data for research purposes. Though researchers have demonstrated the ease with which patient records deidentified using the old method can be re-identified, new rules for deidentification are in process of being developed, and it is quite possible that reidentification concerns will dissipate, making this an extremely attractive option. Hello Health has powerful social media and telemedicine features, and in some states like Maryland legislation allows doctors to be reimbursed for telemedicine; the cost of the visit is far lower than an in-person visit.

Entering the Electronic Age

Practice Fusion gives healthcare providers a no-cost way to use EHRs.

Managed Services Organization

Small physician practices can choose to sign up with a Managed Services Organization (MSO). This concept has been implemented successfully in many states such as Maryland. An MSO serves as the IT department for the doctor's office, and provides hosting and support for many EHR systems. MSOs in Maryland can provide access to certified EHR systems such as Allscripts, Practice Fusion, and others; help train the doctor's office staff; and provide end-user support. They can also ease the transition for the doctor's practice to Meaningful Use, billing, and patient engagement.

EHRs are designed to improve care and reduce costs. With low-cost and free alternatives, even individual practitioners can join the health information technology environment.

EHR Implementations and Results

Several recent conferences allowed me to learn about the results of organizations which have implemented EHRs. At the 2013 CIO Healthcare Summit in Dallas, Jamie Ferguson of Kaiser Permanente discussed the Care Connectivity Consortium, which is advancing the interoperability of care data. The consortium's founders (including Kaiser Permanente) found the FedConnect gateway deficient, so they spent a couple of months writing their own powerful gateway, which is available to the public at no cost.

Phil Fegan described his transition from a chief information officer position to being vice president for excellence in patient care at HealthCare Partners Nevada. He discussed his CEO's vision to drive a single cultural value through the organization -- excellence in patient care. Instead of implementing systems for the convenience of the healthcare provider, he said, providers should focus on convenience for the patient. Healthcare organizations are in business because patients come to them, and as long as patients continue to do so, people in these organizations will have jobs.

Pamela Peele, chief analytics officer of UPMC Health Plan, demonstrated the importance of analytics in improving patient care by analyzing claims data. She explained the difference between reporting and analytics: Reporting is looking at an inventory of what already exists, but analytics is building new information based on what you already have. I thought that was a great distinction. Peele recognized that the claims data she used for analytics had been created for a different purpose, yet it was a rich data set that offered many insights.

She said she likes to hire people who have advanced degrees and are formally trained but are not blinded by their training. Her group uses open-source tools such as GEPHI for showing patterns.

Arvind Kumar of CRICO, the insurer for the Harvard medical institutions, discussed risk mitigation and the reduction of malpractice claims. The insurer has been able to lower the cost of premiums for doctors. Now it has one of the lowest rates of claims paid in the industry. It gives doctors an incentive to improve: Those who meet performance goals get reduced insurance rates. When the insurer sees a problem, it brings all parties together to address the problem.

Finally, Vi Shaffer, an analyst at Gartner, gave us a glimpse into the future, when the model of care is transformed from high-cost, high-risk, and periodic engagement with the patient to persistent, low-cost, and low-risk interaction. "Your e-doctor will see you now," said Shaffer.

A Health Information Technology (HIT) Day organized in early 2013 in Annapolis, Md., by the Maryland chapter of the Health Information Management Systems Society showed me some additional exciting glimpses:

In his opening keynote, Dr. Peter Basch of MedStar Health -- an early adopter and HIT evangelist -- shared his personal experiences and explained how technology has streamlined workflow, fostered patient engagement, and allowed for more comprehensive "shared agenda" patient visits. Though patients may come in for one issue, he said, these visits encompass any and all topics, such as overdue checkups and other health conditions.

Patients are engaged through a patient portal and can see lab results much faster than the traditional means of phone, mail, or fax. Telemedicine costs far less than face-to-face interactions. Technology allows patients to be sent home sooner, improving the quality of care while reducing costs.

Basch highlighted the MedStar Million Hearts campaign, which encourages patients to set achievable health goals to be monitored through technology. Of 68,000 patients seen in a four-month period through this program, 96 percent established blood pressure and cholesterol goals, he said.

Each day, Dr. Barton Leonard of Johns Hopkins Medicine uses the Chesapeake Regional Information System for our Patients (CRISP), Maryland's health information exchange, which is now entering its fifth year of operation. Connected to all hospitals in Maryland, CRISP provides patient records from previous hospitalizations, along with lab and radiology tests and medication history. Authorized professionals access it about 10,000 times a month.

Leonard lauded CRISP for delivering on something that had been discussed for 30 years. He told the story of a young patient who had a life-threatening infection. Time was of the essence, so the first medication *had* to work. Because CRISP housed the patient's complete record, Leonard could quickly choose the most appropriate and effective antibiotic, which saved the patient. As an additional service, CRISP sends 8,500 real-time alerts per month to physicians and care coordinators when patients under their care are hospitalized.

Patient care increasingly is interdisciplinary and collaborative, according to Dr. Andy Barbash of Holy Cross Hospital in Silver Spring. Doctors can engage family members who may be far away -- even on a different continent. Technology often isn't expensive. Barbash recalled one patient who was expecting triplets; unless she got specialized care quickly, she was in danger of losing two of her babies.

The physician used technology to consult with two other doctors and the patient's husband, each in a different city. The best-suited specialist was located via an online search, an appointment was arranged, and the patient was seen -- all in time to ensure the delivery of three healthy babies.

Dr. Neal Reynolds of the University of Maryland Medical System said technology has compressed time and distance and brought doctors and patients closer. In the past, when ambulance crews brought patients to intensive care, they had no idea of the wait time at a particular hospital. Now they are aware of caseloads at the primary location and can be diverted to feeder hospitals, where patients can be treated sooner.

Healthcare legislation at the state level goes hand in hand with the success of HIT. Telemedicine legislation in Maryland allows doctors to get paid for virtual visits. However, it does not address Medicaid reimbursement. Even though 16 states and the District of Columbia have telemedicine bills or laws, additional legislation is needed to allow doctors treating a patient collaboratively across state lines to be paid.

We also need laws that balance the benefits of data sharing and the need to protect privacy to deliver on the promise of improving quality and affordability of healthcare. On the technology side, the public demands improvements such as the ability to choose what portions of a health record can be shared and with whom. Today it is opt in or opt out for the entire patient history. Granularity will be very helpful.

At the 2013 World Health Congress event in Maryland, not only did I get a glimpse of how technology is powering healthcare transformation around the world, I also had the opportunity to meet Nobel peace prize winner and pioneer of micro credit, economist Dr. Muhammad Yunus. Interestingly, his organization is attempting to use the micro-credit concept for healthcare in some US cities.

Dr. Muhammad Yunus and Dr. Mansur Hasib at the speakers reception, World Health Congress 2013, National Harbor, Maryland

John Mackey, co-founder and CEO of Whole Foods described how his company uses technology to engage every employee in a wellness culture by providing financial incentives for health targets and by creating a wellness community through a virtual wellness club.

Dr. Ivan Oransky of Reuters Health (left) and John Mackey of Whole Foods (right) shared a stage -- and laughs. World Health Congress 2013, National Harbor, Maryland

Bryan Sivak, CTO of the US Department of Health and Human Services noted that 70% of the nation's healthcare providers now have electronic health records (EHRs) compared with three years ago, when only 15% had invested in these solutions. Public engagement via a Blue Button, which allows people to download their medical histories, has been very positive, he said.

Shyam Desigan, one of the most strategic CFOs I have met, who also serves as VP of IT at the American Academy of Physician Assistants explained that typical investments in health data analytics pay back in about three years. (Pamela Peele of UPMC Health Plan echoed this estimate.) After listening to Desigan's strategic view of IT investments, I jokingly asked him how he fits in at other events for his CFO peers -- who typically prefer shorter investment payoffs. Desigan laughed and responded, "I don't go to those conferences."

Dr. Geeta Nayyar, chief medical information officer at AT&T, with a dual appointment as assistant clinical professor of medicine at George Washington University, passionately explained her journey incorporating technology into her practice. She discussed how technology has helped her establish a better relationship with clients, improved client access to her, and enhanced patients' health monitoring. Co-panelist Sivak was so impressed he expressed a desire to become Nayyar's patient. Sitting in the audience I had the same feeling -- although my doctor has been embracing EHRs and I expect my doctor's adoption of a patient engagement portal is not far behind.

Ting Shih, CEO and founder of Clickmedix, provided a vision of global telehealth partnerships through technology. The goal is to make healthcare accessible and affordable to everyone in the world.

Vinod Khosla, of Khosla Ventures, delivered a fascinating vision of a future where the best doctors will develop artificial intelligence and diagnosis systems that will improve population health. Technology will replace 80% of what doctors do today, Khosla said. Care will improve, because half of today's doctors are "below average," he said. Physicians are human and have cognitive limitations and cognitive biases. He drove the point home by sharing a statistic. When given detailed diagnoses and asked if patients should get surgery, half the surgeons said yes and half said no. Khosla also provided examples of expensive hospital diagnostic equipment being replaced by inexpensive consumer technology -- similar to the consumerization that has happened for computers and cell phones.

There was a lot of humor, with some of the most enjoyable jokes coming from Dr. Ivan Oransky of Reuters Health, who described the marketing efforts by companies to monetize a health treatment for pre-acne. It's designed to prevent acne before it happens, so the marketing opportunity is from ages zero to twelve -- a huge market. Oransky ended his session by generating great laughter from the audience when he pointed out the opportunity to market to the entire global population, perennially suffering from pre-death!

Delaware Health Information Network

One of the most successful implementations of a health information exchange is the Delaware Health Information Network. Despite an initial round of federal funding to develop state health information exchanges (HIEs) as part of the Affordable Care Act, these clearinghouses were challenged to develop a financially sustainable model. Because it addressed sustainability early, the Delaware Health Information Network is a template for HIE success.

Delaware recognized early on that being a pure exchange would not provide sufficient financial value for hospitals and healthcare providers, Michael Sims, CFO, told me when we met recently at the World Health Congress 2013. In fact, the state's HIE needed to provide services that went far beyond data transport; it had to replace other costly service alternatives for providers so it would be a win for everyone.

DHIN must enroll and engage as many of the Delaware provider population as possible into the HIE. Enrollment meant providers could receive timely and accurate results, which could also be fed into their electronic health records -- thereby optimizing patient care management in an extremely cost-effective way. The HIE planned to pursue volume and drive down the cost per transaction so low that it would be too attractive for physicians and practices to turn down. In fact, DHIN drove down the cost of transactions from about $1.25 each to a mere 25 cents each!

DHIN delivered value to the public and Delaware's healthcare providers by creating a safe and secure data location, with 24x7 accessibility of medical test results and other important health information throughout the state. The organization also created easy to understand communications materials, held regular public meetings, and conducted communications campaigns.

In a follow-up conversation with me, Sims explained that he was fortunate to have acquired the skills to develop non-traditional financial sustainability models during his early experience with startups in the financial sector during the early part of his career.

Randy Farmer, director of provider relations and business development at DHIN, joined the conversation and gave me an overview of DHIN's leadership. Sims and Farmer agreed that one key organizational value shared by the leadership team is "doing the right thing for the citizens of Delaware." Another key value of DHIN is transparency: The HIE welcomes constructive criticism so it can continue fine-tuning and improving its model over time. In my opinion, these two values make a solid foundation for any organization.

In 2007, the Delaware HIE became the first statewide HIE in the country. The market penetration results are impressive: 100 percent of hospitals and long-term care/nursing facilities and almost 100 percent of physicians who make orders are connected to the HIE. The DHIN holds records of 1.4 million people from all 50 states. Growth has been geometric, with 1 percent adoption in 2007, and about 10 percent in 2008 -- until the HIE reached the sustainability tipping point of 42 percent in 2009, Sims said.

Sims and Farmer cited an array of major cost reductions and health benefits, including a 33 percent reduction in high-cost, high-volume lab tests and a 30 percent reduction in radiology tests.

In 2013, DHIN received a $2.48 million innovation grant from the federal government to develop a new model focused on better health and lower costs, the executives told me. DHIN is also reaching out to nearby hospitals in Maryland and looking for collaborative, mutually beneficial partnerships with nearby HIEs such as CRISP in Maryland.

DHIN features a community health record with six years of clinical health records. The Maryland HIE does not have this feature yet. I believe a longitudinal health data warehouse could be a vital resource for states and the nation to help improve public health and reduce healthcare costs. To solve privacy concerns, the data could be de-identified using stronger de-identification techniques that are currently being developed. HIEs could actually generate additional revenue by charging fees for sharing the data warehouse. HIEs could approach foundations interested in various causes to help defray the costs of these investments. It will be very interesting to follow how the DHIN success story continues to unfold.

Overcoming Organizational Issues for IT Governance

We have discussed how IT and cybersecurity governance belongs at the top of any organization. Yet an organization's reporting structure sometimes prevents this from happening. How can we solve this problem?

At a recent Chief Information Security Officer (CISO) summit, Sanjeev Sah, former CISO at the University of North Carolina (UNC) Charlotte, presented an elegant solution. Later I talked with Sah and obtained more details about the model described in this figure:

Taking On the Org Chart

Note: In his presentation on "The Role of IT Governance for Effective Information Security Management" at the CISO Summit in Scottsdale, Ariz. in December, Sanjeev Sah tackled the hierarchical structure and related challenges he's encountered.

In order to be strategic, the CIO and CISO should report to the top layers of an organization. However, history, politics, and personalities frequently cause a sub-optimal organizational structure, which becomes a barrier to strategic IT governance. Changing the organizational structure can be quite difficult. Forming a steering committee that reports to the head of the organization and is empowered to be the strategic body for IT governance can be an effective solution. This is the path UNC Charlotte chose.

When Sah joined UNC Charlotte, he found what is typical in many large universities:

1. The bulk of IT spending distributed across multiple colleges
2. A central IT group and several distributed IT groups within colleges and business units
3. The central IT group controlled roughly 30 percent of the total IT spending at the institution
4. There was no transparency or strategic governance over the bulk of institutional IT spending.

Sah recognized that the institution had to establish an IT governance structure based on the following well-established strategic principle: Business units, guided by institutional mission and priorities, should decide what needs to be done while IT should decide how to do it. As shown in the diagram, Sah envisioned an Information Technology Executive Steering Committee (ITESC) comprised of institutional executive leaders reporting to the Chancellor and the Board of Trustees. ITESC would be advised by an IT Advisory Committee (ITAC), which would also manage the portfolio of IT activities as well as cybersecurity. He and his CIO then evangelized and obtained buy-in for this vision from the rest of the institutional executive leaders.

The result, according to Sah, was been very positive. The ITESC:

- Ensures IT strategic planning is integrated with the university's strategic planning
- Makes IT strategic investment and policy decisions
- Sets campus-wide priorities for IT services, resources, and facilities
- Makes decisions employing a campus-wide funding model that rewards cost-effectiveness and discourages non-strategic IT spending
- Communicates and aligns with the Board of Trustees
- Monitors information security, IT risk management, and regulatory compliance.

The ITAC:

- Assesses and determines strategic fit of proposals
- Performs portfolio reviews and defines project priorities
- Addresses project risks
- Serves as governance, risk, and control sponsor
- Reviews policies
- Ensures IT services are aligned with IT strategy
- Directs execution and integration efforts
- Monitors projects to ensure success
- Oversees IT governance processes.

Several subcommittees advise the ITAC in various domain areas such as services, technology, infrastructure, client interfaces, applications, technology standards and practices, integration, information security, and compliance. Overall, the model engages the entire organization in a cohesive IT and information security governance strategy that is inclusive, transparent, and cost-effective. To me, the model appears promising -- and applicable to many other academic, government, and business organizations that have a need for strategic management of IT spending.

Be Wary of the Amygdala Hijack Condition

While dealing with humans we must realize that all humans have an amygdala. When our amygdala takes hold of our actions, we operate at a significantly lesser mental capacity than we are normally capable of. I have seen even the most seasoned professional fall for social engineering attacks as a result of this phenomenon.

The criminals know this. This is why social engineering attacks where the criminal simply tricks someone into revealing passwords or other confidential information has been so successful. It is also highly pervasive. These attacks are getting more and more sophisticated and harder to detect.

Links and attachments in emails continue to be a major threat to enterprise users. These missives are usually capable of bypassing most antivirus or antispyware systems. Criminals hide behind the anonymity of email and send several thousand emails at a very low cost. They expect that even if a small percentage of their intended victims respond, their financial rewards will be quite large.

Since electronic ordering and billing has become common, sophisticated email scams are on the rise. Recently I received an email asking me to verify my order worth over $900. There was no attachment. There were no obvious grammatical or spelling errors. And there was a helpful, tempting link for me to click.

When I hovered my mouse over the link, I could see that the actual destination was different from the claimed destination in the link. It was a new type of ruse -- quite cleverly prepared.

Though I knew this was a ruse, the email still caused me to go through several emotions in rapid succession -- disbelief, desire to verify, curiosity, desire to rectify the situation, shock, and anger. These are precisely the kinds of reactions that the creators of the ruse had planned to get me to click on the link!

Why did this happen -- and to me, an experienced user? Figuring this out would probably help to explain why people still fall victim to email scams -- and why email continues to be a preferred vehicle for delivering malware.

I think the answer is what one expert calls the "amygdala hijack" -- a primordial reaction that temporarily causes us to relinquish rationality under duress. Road rage is another common example of an amygdala hijack. So is impulsively opening a tempting email or even visiting a tempting website.

So what is the best defense in such a situation?

Remove yourself from the situation immediately before taking any action. You can train yourself to do this every time you face an amygdala hijack condition. You could walk away to get a drink, talk to someone -- essentially giving yourself time away from the situation to think rationally. Once removed from the situation, your rational mind will take over and tell you to simply delete the email -- it is usually the best action.

In addition, one of the best things you can do is talk to someone in cybersecurity. Sometimes even talking to a co-worker may help you relax and react rationally. You may find that many people have received the same email. Your vigilance is likely to help others avoid an amygdala hijack.

Do not expose a co-worker to the threat by forwarding the email. While there is very small probability that some questionable emails will turn out to be legitimate and will have legitimate links, the mere habit of clicking on links and trusting your antivirus or antispyware system to protect you is dangerous. Do not let your curiosity -- or your amygdala -- control your reactions.

It is also very important for cybersecurity strategists to make all their users aware of this amygdala hijack condition so they get in the habit of removing themselves from the event immediately. Then think, discuss rationally with others before taking any type of action.

When Life Tells You to Move On, Listen

No matter how good we are as leaders or how well we served an organization, at regular intervals, we will receive a cue from life: Move on. We should never overstay our welcome. Nor should we lament about what may have happened or try to analyze too much why something happened. We should never blame ourselves or ponder what we could have done different. We cannot undo the past – we must move on and use previous experiences to guide our future.

We fully control our own actions; we have no control over the actions of others. Negativity is like a cancer. If we allow it to take hold, it will kill us. Instead, we should broaden our focus during these junctures. We should explore what else is out there – ask what other adventure could we pursue?

Change is hard. But it is inevitable – specially for innovative and creative leaders. The smaller the organization the sooner we may find ourselves needing to move on because small organizations can exhaust innovative opportunities quickly and enter into a maintenance mode. Long maintenance periods are detrimental for leaders who like to do new things, implement and manage change, and solve problems and issues.

It is impossible to predict when or how these cues will surface but when they do, we will usually feel it. Listening to the cues will usually challenge us and take us to the next higher level in our professional growth – often towards something we had never imagined before.

Every time I got my cue to move on, I did – without ever looking back – and it led to more learning, more adventures, and more fun. The world is full of amazing people and through all my adventures I have met thousands of amazing people and I am very thankful for all my adventures. Every experience – good and bad taught me something.

Sometimes we are compelled to make a change. We need to realize we never control what cards are dealt to us – we just have to play the cards we are dealt, with the highest level of dexterity we can muster. We should never look back – only forward. This is a big world and the opportunities are endless. We have to be brave and optimistic. We need to face the future with an open mind and a big smile. Life will usually smile back.

.

References

Barakat, M. (2001). US Airways loses $766 million in third quarter, worse than analysts expected. *Arlington Journal*, October 31.

Brady, J. W. (2010). *An investigation of factors that affect HIPAA security compliance in academic medical centers.* (Doctoral dissertation). Retrieved from ProQuest Dissertations and Theses. (Order No. 3411810).

Brancatelli, J. (2008). Southwest Airlines' seven secrets for success. Retrieved from http://www.wired.com/cars/futuretransport/news/2008/07/portfoli o_0708

Brown, C. (2005). HIPAA programs: Design and implementation. *Information Systems Security, 14*(1), 10-20. Retrieved from http://www.infosectoday.com/Articles/87267.pdf

Centers for Medicare and Medicaid Services (2012a). *Catalog of minimum acceptable risk controls for Maryland Health Connections – Maryland Health Connection reference architecture supplement.* Centers for Medicare and Medicaid Services, Baltimore: MD.

Centers for Medicare and Medicaid Services (2012b). *Harmonized security and privacy framework – Maryland Health Connection reference architecture supplement.* Centers for Medicare and Medicaid Services, Baltimore: MD.

Corriss, L. (2010). *Information security governance: Integrating security into the organizational culture.* Proceedings of the Governance of Technology, Information and Policy, 26th Annual Computer Security Applications Conference, 7 December, 2010, 35-41. United States Military Academy, West Point, New York: NY.

Dark, M. J., Ekstrom, J. J., & Lunt, B. M. (2006). Integration of information assurance and security into the IT2005 curriculum. *Journal of Information Technology Education, 5*, 389-402.

Davey, B., McEveety, S, & Wallace, R. (Producers), & Wallace, R. (Director). (2002). *We were soldiers* [Motion picture]. USA: Paramount Pictures.

Deal, T. E., & Kennedy, A. A. (1982). *Corporate cultures: The rites and rituals of corporate life.* Reading, MA: Addison-Wesley.

Dutta, A., & McCrohan, K. (2002). Management's role in information security in a cyber economy. *California Management Review, 45*(1), 67-87.

Embse, T. J. V. D., Desai, M. S., & Ofori-Brobbey, K. (2010). A new perspective on ethics safeguards: Where is the clout? *S.A.M. Advanced Management Journal*, *75*(3), 4-10, 51.

Gitell, J. H. , Cameron, K, & Lim, S.G.P. (2005). Relationships, layoffs, and organizational resilience: Airline industry responses to September 11ᵗʰ. Retrieved from http://www.bus.umich.edu/positive/PDF/Gittell%20Cameron%20Li m-Org%20Resilience%20Jan%2005.pdf

Hasib, M. (2010, March). *Information Technology 2.0 in Higher Education*. Conference presentation at Innovations 2010. League for Innovation, Baltimore: MD.

Hasib, M., Swartz, D., Finn, L. (2011, January). *CIOs: What You Need to Know to Be One, or to Work for One*. Conference presentation at Educause Mid-Atlantic Conference. Educause, Baltimore, MD.

Hasib, M. (2012, March). *Securing proprietary information in healthcare: human controls*. Paper presented at Healthcare CIO Summit 2012. CDMMedia, Scottsdale: AZ.

Hasib, M. (2013, March). *Success in the IT Field: B's Are Also Important*. Keynote speech at Honors Convocation 2013. Capitol College, Laurel: MD.

Hasib, M. (2013). *Impact of security culture on security compliance in healthcare in the United States of America*. Laurel, MD: Capitol College.

Hassell, L., & Wiedenbeck, S. (2004). *Human factors and information security*. Retrieved from http://repository.binus.ac.id/content/A0334/A033461622.pdf

HIMSS Analytics (2008). *2008 HIMSS analytics report: Security of patient data commissioned by Kroll Fraud Solutions*. Retrieved from http://www.mmc.com/views/Kroll_HIMSS_Study_April2008.pdf

HIMSS Analytics (2010). *2010 HIMSS analytics report: Security of patient data commissioned by Kroll Fraud Solutions*. Retrieved from http://www.krollfraudsolutions.com/about-kroll/himss-security-patient-data-report.aspx

HIMSS Analytics (2012). *2012 HIMSS analytics report: Security of patient data commissioned by Kroll Advisory Solutions*. Retrieved from http://www.krollcybersecurity.com/media/Kroll-HIMSS_2012_-_Security_of_Patient_Data_040912.pdf

Internal Revenue Service (2014). Publication 1075. Retrieved from http://www.irs.gov/pub/irs-pdf/p1075.pdf

John, L. K. (2011). CIO: Concept is over. *Journal of Information Technology*, *26*(2), 129-138. doi: http://dx.doi.org/10.1057/jit.2011.4

Li, J., & Shaw, M. J. (2008). Electronic medical records, HIPAA, and patient privacy. *International Journal of Information Security and Privacy*, *2*(3), 45-54.

Maconachy, W. V., Schou, C. D., Ragsdale, D., & Welch, D. (2001). *A model for information assurance: An integrated approach*. Proceedings of the 2001 IEEE Workshop on Information Assurance and Security, 5-6 June, 2001, 306-310. United States Military Academy, West Point, New York: NY.

McAdams, A. C. (2004). Security and risk management: A fundamental business issue. *Information Management Journal, 38*(4), 36-44.

Mercuri, R. T. (2004). The HIPAA-potamus in health care data security. *Communications of the ACM, 47*(7), 25-28. doi:10.1145/1005817.1005840

Parker, J. (2010). CEO@Smith: Jim Parker. Robert H. Smith Business School, University of Maryland. Lecture Feb 24, 2010. Retrieved from http://www.rhsmith.umd.edu/news/stories/2010/CEOatSmith-Parker.aspx

Parker, J. F. (2008). *Do the right thing*. Upper Saddle River, NJ: Wharton School.

Ponemon Institute (2009, January). *2008 annual study: Cost of a data breach*. Retrieved from http://www.ponemon.org/local/upload/fckjail/generalcontent/18/file/2008-2009%20US%20Cost%20of%20Data%20Breach%20Report%20Final.pdf

Probst, C. W., Hunker, J., Gollman, D., & Bishop, M. (2010). *Insider threats in cyber security*. New York, NY: Springer Science.

Ross, S. R., Kirsch, L. J., Angermeier, I., Shingler, R. A. & Boss, R. W. (2009). If someone is watching, I'll do what I'm asked: Mandatoriness, control, and information security. *European Journal of Information Systems, 18*, 151-164. doi:10.1057/ejis.2009.8

Rossen, R. (Producer), & Rossen, R. (Director). (1949). *All the king's men* [Motion picture]. USA: Columbia Pictures.

Schlienger, T., & Teufel, S. (2003). Information security culture: From analysis to change. *South African Computer Journal, 31*, 46-52.

Sorrell, J. (2012, November 9). Ethics: The Patient Protection and Affordable Care Act: Ethical Perspectives in 21st Century Health Care. *OJIN: The Online Journal of Issues in Nursing, 18*(1)

Southwest.com (2012a). Retrieved from http://www.southwest.com/html/cs/landing/bags_flyfree.html

Southwest.com, (2012b) Southwest Airlines has Acquired AirTran. Retrieved from: http://www.southwest.com/html/about-southwest/lowfaresfarther.html

The Daily Beast (2010, February 4). Lay off the layoffs. Retrieved from http://www.thedailybeast.com/newsweek/2010/02/04/lay-off-the-layoffs.html

Tuckman, B. W. (1965). *Psychological Bulletin, 63*(6), 384-399

United States Department of Health and Human Services (2002). *Standards for privacy of individually identifiable health information: Final rule.* Retrieved from http://www.gpo.gov/fdsys/pkg/FR-2002-08-14/pdf/02-20554.pdf

United States Department of Health and Human Services (2003). *Health insurance reform security standard: Final rule.* Retrieved from http://www.hhs.gov/ocr/privacy/hipaa/administrative/securityrule/securityrulepdf.pdf

Weber, B., Alcaro, B., & Ciotti, V. (2001). Avoiding HIPAA hype: Preparing for HIPAA affordably. *Healthcare Financial Management, 55*(8), 62-65.

Westby, J. R., Allen, J. H. (2007). *Governing for enterprise security (GES) implementation guide.* Retrieved from http://www.cert.org/archive/pdf/07tn020.pdf

White, G. (2009). Strategic, tactical, & operational management security model. *The Journal of Computer Information Systems, 49*(3), 71-75.

Index

ABOUT THE AUTHOR

Dr. Mansur Hasib, CISSP, PMP, CPHIMS
Cybersecurity Leader, Keynote Speaker, Author, and Media Commentator
2017 Cybersecurity People's Choice Award Winner

Dr. Mansur Hasib is the only cybersecurity and healthcare leader, author, speaker, and media commentator in the world with 12 years experience as Chief Information Officer, a Doctor of Science in Cybersecurity (IA), and the prestigious CISSP, PMP, and CPHIMS certifications. Dr. Hasib has 30 years experience in leading organizational transformations through digital leadership and cybersecurity strategy in healthcare, biotechnology, education, and energy. Dr. Hasib currently teaches the art of cybersecurity leadership, digital innovation and strategy to graduate students and executives worldwide and is Program Chair of the graduate Cybersecurity Technology program at UMUC. He is also a cybersecurity faculty at UMBC.

With a Bachelor's degree in Economics and Politics and a Master's degree in Political Science, Dr. Hasib has a unique interdisciplinary perspective and can discuss poetry and culture as comfortably as digital strategy, business innovation, and cybersecurity. He is the author of Cybersecurity Leadership: Powering the Modern Organization (ebook, paperback, and audio), which received two nominations for The Cybersecurity Canon 2016 – the Hall of Fame for cybersecurity books. He conducted a national study of US healthcare cybersecurity and published the book Impact of Security Culture on Security Compliance in Healthcare in the USA. He has also published Muses and Rhymes – a collection of poems he wrote as a youth.
Dr. Hasib enjoys table tennis, comedy, and travel and has been to all 50 states of the USA.
Follow him on Twitter @mhasib or
LinkedIn http://www.linkedin.com/in/mansurhasib.
To contact Dr. Hasib visit:
www.cybersecurityleadership.com

Made in the USA
Middletown, DE
12 January 2020